LIVING THE GOSPEL in the GREY

THE ART OF COMING ALONGSIDE

by Rob Schrumpf
in collaboration with Jason Tennenhouse

Cover art and interior art by Garrett Curry
Title design by Emily Knapp

CONTENTS

Gospel in Motion

[An Introduction to What Follows]

When I was young, I remember watching as my mother took oil painting classes. Her early masterpieces were in a genre called "still life," wherein, for example, a bowl of fruit would be placed on a table in the middle of a room full of aspiring artists and each would simply paint what she saw from her unique vantage point.

Translate that metaphor to the subject of what it means to share the Gospel and you can understand the reasons for so many different approaches. The multiplicity of books, programs, resources, conferences, sermons, curricula, DVD series, workshops, dramas, retreats, and the like have depicted evangelism from various perspectives and angles of theology and methodology. It's the same basic message, but each person has a different perspective.

The purpose of this book is neither to offer the "new and improved" method of evangelism, nor to diminish the critical need to share the Gospel. The intention is not to nudge another proverbial canvas into the room in order to express one more version of the "still-life portrait of evangelism." Rather, I would like to question the premise that there is anything even remotely "still" or static about the Gospel, or the sharing of it; evangelism cannot be reduced to a list of constant strategies over time and space.

The Gospel is too important to keep quiet, but in our fondness for systems and formulaic templates, we have often sacrificed the beautiful and frustrating complexities of relational ministry and intentional godliness for the step-by-step instructions and canned rhetoric of the latest evangelistic methods. The following pages hopefully will be less like a "still life" that can be painted, analyzed, and reproduced, and more like a series of photographs that capture the sometimes-blurry images of the Gospel in motion.

This book is more like a journal or memoir and less like an instructional treatise, and my hope is that it comes from a place of honesty rather than narcissism. I have spent the last twenty-five years on a college campus trying to figure out what it means to share and live the Gospel, mostly feeling like a failure because the proposed rubric of evangelistic formulas and instructional guides have always seemed foreign to me. Simply put, this is my attempt to come to grips with the ambiguous concept of evangelism.

Although my frame of reference is the university setting, my hope is that Jesus followers of all ages and demographics would be stretched and encouraged through these words. It is a collection of thoughts and experiences, a wrestling through questions of motivation and of how to love people well. Traces can be glimpsed here of other, more astute writers and thinkers who have influenced and shaped my perspective over the years, to whom I feel a deep debt and with whom I would love to have a cup of coffee. The fingerprints of many are all over these pages: Peterson, Keller, Fischer, Peacock, Giglio, Allender, McKinley, Edwards, as well as a plethora of university students, the Campus House staff, my incredible eighty-year-old parents, and friends like Dave Shockey who have continued to influence these words.

I must mention three people in particular who have both inspired and shaped my thoughts. First, there's my wife, Lea, whose life epitomizes the concept of "coming alongside" with raw honesty and grace (a self-proclaimed introvert who once had a forty-five-minute conversation/counseling session with a telemarketer who was going through a rough time—just saying). I am so grateful to get to do life and ministry alongside her. Secondly, I want to say thanks to my friend, Jason Hendrick, who I describe as a pastor disguised as a doctor. He not only routinely speaks truth into my life, but has also made a huge impact on our community in the way he takes the whole Gospel to the whole person—spiritually, physically, and emotionally.

Finally, the other name on the cover belongs to Jason Tennenhouse who, for almost a decade, has led our ministry and been the creative force behind much of our community outreach and mobilization, including Greyhouse, GreyMob, Starry Night, and this book project. Over the years, we have wrestled through a lot of these thoughts via conversations, prayer, and simply trying to keep in step with God's Spirit, and I am thankful for his friendship and encouragement along the way.

Here is what I hope you get out of this book: First, the knowledge that the authentic sharing of the Gospel flows out of a life that has been transformed by Jesus. And second, the desire that as we internalize and are shaped by His grace and truth, "Christ in us" will inevitably become "Christ through us" to a world desperate for love. The context for this is in the grey. The grey is outside the safe and predictable, beyond the scripted and "three easy steps" realm we so often inhabit. The grey is about engaging neighbors and culture where life is messy, unpredictable, and rather hazy. Jesus is up to something in the grey. May He give us eyes to see it.

JESUS IS UP TO
SOMETHING IN THE
GREY. MAY HE GIVE
US EYES TO SEE IT.

Chapter One

A Matter of Perspective

[Evangelism from Both Sides of the Glass]

After worship one Sunday, two of our male students burst into my office, barely able to contain their excitement. Just the night before, they had been at a party and had struck up a conversation with a girl who obviously needed to talk. Reluctant at first, she finally revealed that she was going through a tough time and was dealing with a lot of brokenness. While the music blared in the other room, the guys shared the Gospel message with her and it was a life-changing experience. Through her tears, she prayed to receive Christ, and they left the party elated that God had used them to lead this girl to the Lord.

Later that week, one of our female students burst into my office, barely able to contain her frustration. She was livid as she shared how her roommate had been (in her words) "accosted by two Christian guys at a party." They had been determined to convert her but had only proceeded to confuse and upset her to the point of tears. She had finally agreed to pray a "sinner's prayer" (their words), but from the perspective of the girl, it was more a prayer of "I'll say this so you'll get off my back" than a prayer of repentance to receive salvation.

The story gets even more tragic. In the weeks leading up to the party, this girl had been opening up to her Christian roommate, having honest conversations and asking thoughtful questions about faith and God and life. After this experience, however, she made it clear that she wanted nothing to do with Christianity or the late-night talks.

I hate that story. The two guys weren't being jerks. They are two of the most on-fire, sincere followers of Christ that I know. But on this particular night, their zeal for evangelism got in the way of their ability to actually share the Gospel. In the midst of trying to save the girl, they missed the girl. In a very real sense, it became more about them than about her.

How does that happen? Why are people so often drowned by the very Christians trying to rescue them? Why has the word "evangelism" become synonymous with gimmicks, manipulation, and burned bridges? Has our collective perspective and motivation become skewed?

Before I propose some ideas and stories about what sharing the Good News might look like, let me pose a few questions and illustrations to help deconstruct what I see as a distorted perspective of evangelism.

ARE WE TAKING AN INSINCERE INTEREST IN SOMEONE JUST SO HE OR SHE WILL BECOME A CHRISTIAN?

We bought some kitchen appliances from a big appliance store. The salesman spent a long time with us and seemed truly interested in our family and our story. He told us about his grandkids, helped us find a refrigerator, and pretended not to care that my little boy was testing out the vacuum cleaners. He was the nicest guy in the world. A couple of days later, we went back to the store and it was as if he had never laid eyes on us, asking, "Now who are you again?"

Many people have told me similar stories about "salesmen-like" believers who were more interested in sealing the deal than in building a relationship. There is nothing less authentic than a Christian who turns on the charm to make you a deal you can't refuse.

ARE WE EVANGELIZING TO HELP OUR REPUTATION WITH CHURCH PEOPLE OR OUR STANDING WITH GOD?

My kids' school has multiple fundraisers each year and if a child sells $200 worth of candy or popcorn or first-aid kits, he gets points that can be used toward valuable items like a troll head pencil topper. Similarly, sharing the Good News of Christ to collect a prize (whether gold stars or compliments or reputation) misses the heart of the Gospel completely.

ARE WE PROPONENTS OF BAIT AND SWITCH?

I got a call from a representative of a group that wanted to bring an evangelistic event to our campus. That isn't really our favorite method of outreach, but we want to be supportive of other ministries so I agreed to meet with him. He brought a sample of a poster they intended to use for advertising the event. The poster read: "THE event of the year! Come out for [famous band] and a nationally known speaker." There was nothing on the poster about the fact that this was a Christian thing, let alone that the speaker was going to give a "Gospel presentation." I asked the guy how non-Christians feel when they show up at these events and realize it is not what was advertised. The guy said, "I never thought about it that way." Exactly.

ARE WE TRYING TO GET THE UPPER HAND IN A CONVERSATION TO WIN THE ARGUMENT OR EMBARRASS SOMEONE ELSE?

I overheard this conversation: "Did you see that debate last night? The Christian guy made the Muslim guy look like a fool. The poor guy was flustered and didn't know what to say. [The Christian guy] definitely won the debate."

Is it really about winning the debate? Is our goal in taking a stand for the truth to embarrass people? Are we trying to scare or manipulate or guilt someone into the Kingdom?

Some folks in America use evangelistic tools that are a bit abusive. There are several examples to choose from: walking kids through a simulated hell, B-movies about the apocalypse, staging terrorist takeovers of churches to see who will denounce God in order to not be shot. Crazy stuff. One well-known, slightly less scarring method is to ask the following question, "If you were to die tonight, do you know where you would spend eternity?" It's a legitimate question, I guess, but it does two things:

1. It uses fear as the primary motivation to convince someone to stay out of hell and get into heaven.

2. It says nothing about what happens if you don't "die tonight."

If you don't die tonight, is there another way to live? Abrasive tactics might get someone to say the sinner's prayer but do little to introduce them to the One who created them, died for them, and offers them true hope and freedom.

One final question:

DO WE GENERALLY FEEL LIKE FAILURES, FAKERS, OR DRIVEN BY FEAR WHEN WE THINK ABOUT EVANGELISM?

You may be familiar with this passage:

> **"Therefore go and make disciples of all nations, baptizing them in the name of the Father and of the Son and of the Holy Spirit, and teaching them to obey everything I have commanded you. And surely I am with you always, to the very end of the age."**
>
> *(Matthew 28:19–20 NIV)*

For a believer, these words of Jesus are not optional, right? It's a commission—a mandate. Because of that, for a lot of years I wrestled with the guilt-inducing expectation that I should be sharing my faith with people a whole lot more than I was. I had friends for whom, it seemed, evangelism was as effortless as breathing. They would be ordering waffles and ten minutes later the waitress would be praying to receive Christ. When I tried, it never came out right.

For instance, I played football in high school and determined it would be a "witnessing opportunity" if, should I happen to score a touchdown, I would kneel in prayer in the end-zone, offering thanks to God for the six points and returning to the sideline to see my teammates and coaches in tears asking, "What should we do to be saved?" as the marching band played "Just As I Am"—the game pausing as fans poured out of the stands and onto the field to accept Christ, saying, "There is Gatorade. What prevents me from being baptized?" At least, that's how it played out in my imagination.

In reality, I did score a touchdown, awkwardly knelt in the end-zone and prayed a prayer of thanks. But when I returned to the sideline, I was greeted with, "Hey Schrumpf! Did you lose a contact, or what? What the &%#! were you doing out there?"

So much for making disciples of all nations. I couldn't even convert the water boy. I was at an evangelism conference in Cincinnati a few years later, and one day our assignment was to go to a particular section of town and knock on doors to tell people about Christ. I looked for houses that appeared to have no one home so I could leave a note and church information on the door without actually having to talk to anybody.

Somewhere along the line I missed the point of the Great Commission. I missed the part about evangelism being about loving people and serving people, about listening to people and connecting them to Christ rather than simply meeting a quota.

There is another way. Peter and Paul transition us from minimalistic, formulaic, fear- and guilt-driven "evangelism" to the art of sharing and being the Gospel.

> **"Do not fear what they fear. Do not be frightened. But in your hearts set apart Christ as Lord. Always be prepared to give an answer to everyone who asks you to give the reason for the hope that you have. But do this with gentleness and respect..."**
>
> *(1 Peter 3:14–15 NIV)*

> **"Because we loved you so much, we were delighted to share with you not only the gospel of God but our lives as well."**
>
> *(1 Thessalonians 2:8 NIV)*

One night my friend asked me to tell him about my faith. For a couple of hours I unpacked the whole story, but I think an essential part of the conversation was telling him that regardless of whether he accepted Christ or not, I was still going to be his friend. I also told him that I would be a lousy friend if I didn't share with him the most important thing in my life. The tension between those two statements is the crux of this book:

- Loving and serving people without conditions or agendas, and building the trust and validity to speak truth into their lives.

- Not making demands of people to clean up their acts and come into our buildings and participate in our programs, but meeting them on their terms, in their space, in their timing with credible intentionality.

THE BEST WAY I HAVE FOUND TO SAY IT IS WITH THE PHRASE: "THE ART OF COMING ALONGSIDE."

Road trips have always been in my blood. We traveled a ton when I was growing up, and upon graduation, I chose a college eight hundred miles away from home, partially because I enjoy a good road trip. My wife and I have taken the family on vacations to the beach in Florida, to the mountains in Colorado, and to my sister's house in Maine, all of which are twenty-four-hour trips by car. (We live in Indiana so any excuse to see mountains or sand is worth the forced "family bonding" of a long ride.)

When a person travels a long distance, there is a relational thing that happens on the highway. Sometimes you journey in a "pod" of fellow travelers, all moving at a similar speed and in the same direction, like migrating whales. If you're like me, you develop some assumptions about your fellow nomads.

For instance, you draw conclusions about the minivan from California carrying a family that obviously needs Jesus because their child keeps sticking her tongue out at you, or the semi-truck driver conversing on his CB radio, likely gossiping to all of his truck driver friends about the awful paint job you gave your van in an attempt to cover up the rust.

You make assumptions about the middle-aged man with the comb-over, reliving the age of Metallica, simultaneously attempting to drive his car and perform a ripping solo on his air guitar. After a few miles, you get to "know" these people—and not only are you making up stories about them, but you also develop a symbiotic relationship. You block for each other so that your traveling buddy can change lanes effortlessly. Their brake lights warn you of speed traps and wayward animals. You come to rely on them as if the interstate is somehow a safer, more pleasant place because of this group of fellow sojourners.

The point is that you merge onto a road already filled with travelers; you journey together for a period of time, until someone in your van has a full bladder and you take the next off-ramp, feeling rather sad to leave your newfound friends.

When it comes to sharing the Gospel, the essence of this "coming alongside" journey is similar. Sometimes it is a twenty-minute conversation, and sometimes a twenty-year friendship; but when it comes to sharing the truth and love of God with somebody, we are joining something already in progress. God has already started sharing His truth and love with that person since the day they were born. We simply join the conversation—we come alongside and help clear the ground where decisions are made.

In this process, God calls us to live distinctively, love intentionally, and share not only the words of the Gospel, but our lives as well. It is a form of art in that it takes creativity and improvisation, patience and passion, instinct and perception.

John starts his letter to the churches with these words:

"That which was from the beginning, which we have heard, which we have seen with our eyes, which we have looked at and our hands have touched—this we proclaim concerning the Word of life."

(1 John 1:1 NIV)

Our starting point is what we have heard, seen, and touched—our story about His Story. When our experiences are aligned with the lens of the Word, we simply tell the truth about the Truth.

CONSIDER THIS
A Matter of Perspective

1. What do you think of when you hear the word "evangelism?" What is your gut reaction?

2. Have you ever seen or experienced "evangelism" that has included disingenuous pretending, earning bragging rights or points with others, bait and switch, winning a debate, or laying a guilt trip on someone? If so, what was your response? Which of these substitutes or simplifications do you find yourself most tempted to employ?

3. Why do we so often reduce evangelism to what is safe or formulaic?

4. What aspects of the Gospel's truth and transforming power are lost in these overly simplified reductions?

5. Have you ever interacted with anyone in your life for whom evangelism seemed effortless? What was your emotional response to watching this person? Guilt? Respect? Awe? Or did it make you want to slash their tires?

6. What preconceived notions, attitudes, familiarities, or negative experiences do you need to prayerfully suspend in order to view the Gospel in motion?

WHEN OUR
EXPERIENCES ARE
ALIGNED WITH
THE LENS OF THE
WORD, WE SIMPLY
TELL THE TRUTH
ABOUT THE TRUTH.

Chapter Two

Witness Redefined

[Experiencing the Story Yourself]

I once was a witness to a crime. My wife and I were getting ready for bed very late one night when we heard an incredibly loud car making its way through the neighborhood. Two things were obvious: One, the car had no muffler, and two, the driver had no scruples about waking the good folks on Stanforth Avenue in the middle of the night. To make things more obnoxious, the car kept circling the block. After several orbits, my patience was on empty, and in my frustrated state, I decided to report the mayhem to the local authorities. I dialed 9-1-1 and walked out onto the front porch as the dispatcher picked up.

Dispatcher: "9-1-1."

Me: "I would like to report a suspicious automobile."

Dispatcher: "Can you describe the automobile, sir?"

Me: "It's loud."

Dispatcher: "Can you be a little more specific, sir?"

Just then, the muffler-deprived car turned onto our street and stopped directly in front of our house. That's when I began to feel a bit vulnerable. Standing on a well-lit porch in my boxers, I attempted to crouch down in the shadows as I gave the second-by-second update to Pseudo-annoyed Dispatch Lady.

Me [whispering into the phone]: "The car just stopped in front of my house."

At that exact moment, a kid—who by the way had been hiding in our bushes just six feet away and who had been listening as I played McGruff the Crime-fighting Dog, stumbled out of the bushes with a purse in his hand and made a dash to the idling get-away car.

Me: "A high school kid was hiding in the bushes just six feet away from me and just ran and got in the car."

Dispatcher: "Well, perhaps you can get the license plate number."

And I did. I ran out into the street. The gangsters had sped off into the night, but not before I memorized the license plate number, spouted it off to the dispatcher, and returned to bed with my heart racing.

I couldn't sleep.

The police stopped by at about 3:00 a.m. to say "thanks for the tip." They had caught the bad guys and it turned out (as I had suspected) that the purse hadn't really belonged to the high school boy at all, but rather to my neighbor who had left it in an unlocked car. In fact, the juvies had a trunk full of loot they had "borrowed" from the sleeping people of our unsuspecting neighborhood.

After they left, a couple of thoughts went through my head. One was that I felt a sense of pride for being such a model citizen. I entertained instant daydreams about being honored by the mayor for saving the town, him presenting me with a plaque and the key to the city, and my picture on the front page of the paper with the caption: "Heroic Campus Minister Snatches Purse Thief."

That thought, however, was followed by this one: "Those guys I just busted know exactly where I live."

Crap.

And then my mind exploded into a thousand scenarios and contingency plans for protecting my family. I had thoughts about getting a security system or having snipers posted on the neighbor's roof or entering the witness relocation program and having to grow a long beard and moving my family to Des Moines or Finland.

The reality is that these guys weren't part of the mob; they were just juvenile wannabes who might have had the capacity to teepee our house. But still, I had those thoughts. I realized through this experience why every episode of *Law and Order, NCIS*, or *CSI Miami* has a reluctant witness as part of the plot: speaking the truth about what we see might cost us something valuable.

Being a witness is all-encompassing. It is costly. It is honest. It is not compartmentalized. It is not simply something you do—it is who you are.

> **"But you will receive power when the Holy Spirit comes on you; and you will be my witnesses in Jerusalem, and in all Judea and Samaria, and to the ends of the earth."**
> *(Acts 1:8 NIV)*

Contrary to popular belief, Scripture never uses the phrase "going witnessing," as if attesting to the love of God was something we could sell door to door, or turn on or off, or put in our schedule a couple of times a month. The Gospel was never intended to be compartmentalized into a task to be checked off the list or used to subtly (or not so subtly) build one's spiritual resumé. "You will be my witnesses . . ."

Our state of being a witness flows out of not only what Christ has done, but also what He is doing. On the one hand, Jesus is the same yesterday, today, and forever. Scripture is clear that there can be only one foundation, one meta-narrative that is eternal and unchanging. However, our interaction with Jesus, the way our story of brokenness is woven around His Story of redemption, continues to be written and stretched, built, and restored. This is what we "bear witness to" in the day-to-day, moment-by-moment offering of our lives.

Okay. So we are witnesses. What does that look like?

Please turn in your Bibles to the Book of Revelation.

John's vision has been used by many to inspire evangelistic efforts (i.e., scare the hell out of church people so they can, in turn, scare the hell out of unchurched people). But if we could transcend, for a moment, the desire to postulate which world leader is quite possibly the antichrist, in the middle of the book there are some interesting things that extrapolate this notion of being a witness.

Please feel free to read the backstory, but in chapter 10, John is attempting to describe the indescribable.

> **"Then I saw another mighty angel coming down from heaven. He was robed in a cloud, with a rainbow above his head; his face was like the sun, and his legs were like fiery pillars. He was holding a little scroll, which lay open in his hand. He planted his right foot on the sea and his left foot on the land, and he gave a loud shout like the roar of a lion. When he shouted, the voices of the seven thunders spoke. And when the seven thunders spoke, I was about to write; but I heard a voice from heaven say, 'Seal up what the seven thunders have said and do not write it down.'"**
>
> *(Revelation 10:1–4 NIV)*

Being a good journalist, John is there ready to record the scene. "Seven thunders—most impressive." But then he is told to turn off his laptop. John is told to refrain from revealing the words, not with the intention of withholding truth, but because the world wasn't ready to hear them. John had been given a similar command on the Mount of Transfiguration[1] when he, his brother, and the perpetually tactless Peter, were told to keep the experience to themselves. Jesus in His glorified form, hanging out with Elijah and Moses, was a lot to keep quiet and the scene was obviously recorded later in the Gospels, but coming down from the mountain, they were to keep silent. It was not yet time for the world to know these things.

25

Evidently when it comes to being a witness to the grace and goodness of God, there is a time to speak and a time to be quiet.

If our goal is not just trying to get people into heaven, but having a desire for them to experience God's wholeness in their lives now, then we need to listen. People certainly need to be saved from an eternity in hell but they also need to be saved from the form of hell they experience from not knowing God presently. They need to be saved from the confusion of their emotional roller-coasters. They need to be healed from past abuse. They need to know that there really is a way out of their addictions. They need somebody who cares enough to listen to their doubts, questions, and rants, who will love them in the midst of their brokenness and pain. They need a Jesus follower who is honest about his or her own messiness and who gives more than hopeful words. They need someone who is willing to engage with silence, to stay present, to listen.

THE VISION GOES ON

In the next few verses, the angel raises his hand and makes a promise that the bad news from previous chapters—things like hail and fire, falling stars and blackened sun, locusts and the annihilation of humanity—that kind of bad news—is not God's last word.

"There will be no more delay! But in the days when the seventh angel is about to sound his trumpet, the mystery of God will be accomplished, just as he announced to his servants the prophets."
(Revelation 10:6–7 NIV)

To transform bad news to good news, John must be drawn into the story and that story leaves him assuming an appropriate smallness.

> **"Then the voice that I had heard from heaven spoke to me once more: 'Go, take the scroll that lies open in the hand of the angel who is standing on the sea and on the land.' So I went to the angel and asked him to give me the little scroll."**
>
> *(Revelation 10:8–9 NIV)*

Back in chapter 5, John mentioned a scroll that only Jesus can open, but apparently this is a smaller, CliffsNotes version. Even the condensed version is beyond comprehension. John, being prepared to be a "witness," is given this Gospel that is deeply beautiful and complex, both transcendent and immanent.

John could identify with Job who claimed that we are only on the outskirts of God's power, on the fringe of God's ways.

> **"These are just the beginning of all that he does, merely a whisper of his power."**
>
> *(Job 26:14 NLT)*

Whatever we say about the Gospel, it's only a minute brushstroke on the mural of God's huge Story. No matter how well we say it, we're like a four-year-old trying to describe quantum physics. But our inadequacy is exactly what God wants to use. In our attempts to verbalize the Good News, God makes up for what gets lost in translation. His Spirit fills in the gaps.

Let me give you an example.

I was in Matamoros, Mexico, a few years ago where, along with a group of college students, we were building a house for a family. On a break, I went to their version of a 7/11 to buy some awesome Jarritos Mandarin Soda. I took a translator with me because my Spanish is, well, non-existent, and as we shopped together for the sugary orange beverage, the two of us started talking with the owner of the shop. In the midst of our conversation, she shared (through the interpreter) her story, her brokenness, and the need for something to change in her life. I began to simply tell her that God loved her very much, that He knew the depths of her pain and loneliness, and that through Jesus, He desired to enter the chaos and give her forgiveness and life.

Now, how this interpretation thing was supposed to work is that the translator was simply supposed to translate my words into Spanish and her words into English, but that's not how it worked in practice. He cheated. Instead, I would say a sentence and then translator guy would say three paragraphs, and the shopkeeper's eyes would widen, and her face would light up with a smile. I would ask him what he just said to her, and his response would be: "I just said what you said. Plus a bit more."

The woman made a decision to follow Jesus that day and we connected her with a local group of Jesus followers. I also had the opportunity to understand a little of what it means to come alongside and participate in what the Holy Spirit is up to.

Whatever words we can muster are usually few and jumbled and fairly unintelligible. But the Translator fills in and around them with fluid expressions of truth and substance and beauty in the exact dialect of that person. He knows their wiring, their experiences, their struggles, their doubts, their questions, their hang-ups, and their pasts. He knows them, having knit them together, and since their birth has been in pursuit of their hearts.

God is calling us to love people, to listen, to serve, to preach the Gospel, and to use words with the full assurance that God's Spirit will affirm, animate, and amplify those words.

We take a stab at communicating this Gospel. The Holy Spirit backs us up. The truth of Christ penetrates to the hardest of hearts; not because of our eloquence, knowledge, or charisma, but because God, in His vast power and "beyondness" has intimately changed our lives and, in His grace, has given us a new story.

In this awareness, we recognize what John knew—there is a humility that comes with being a witness. There is also ownership. I quote this verse a lot from Philippians:

> **"And if on some point you think differently, that too God will make clear to you. Only let us live up to what we have already attained."**
>
> *(Philippians 3:15–16 NIV)*

"I JUST DON'T KNOW ENOUGH."

Welcome to the club. Fortunately, there is not a prerequisite to have a ton of knowledge or decades of experience before you share the Gospel. Speak, listen, serve, and live out of what you do know.

> **The angel continues, "He said to me, 'Take it and eat it. It will turn your stomach sour, but in your mouth it will be as sweet as honey.' I took the little scroll from the angel's hand and ate it. It tasted as sweet as honey in my mouth, but when I had eaten it, my stomach turned sour. Then I was told, 'You must prophesy again about many peoples, nations, languages and kings.'"**
>
> *(Revelation 10:9–11 NIV)*

"EAT THESE WORDS."

Chew on them. Internalize them. Experience them. Believe them. Live them. The grace and truth of Jesus must become a part of us before we speak about them. This is the essence of what it means to witness. When "witnessing" becomes compartmentalized, programmed, or in any way separate from the whole of our lives, hypocrisy is revealed. People aren't stupid. They can sense when they are some sort of project rather than a friend.

My friend Tim called from a gas station after his car broke down on the interstate. Tim is a friendly guy so while he was waiting for me to come pick him up, he engaged in a conversation with a woman who was seemingly waiting for a ride as well.

Tim: "So did your car break down too?"

Woman: "No. No, it didn't."

There was then a change in the woman's countenance, a kind of a glowing with a sparkle in her eyes and a toothy smile. She looked Tim in the eye and said,

Woman: "But if it had, I know that God would have taken care of me. Do you know Jesus Christ as your personal Lord and Savior?"

Tim: "Why, yes. Yes, I do."

Now there was another change in the woman's countenance. The glow faded, any sparkle was snuffed, and the toothy grin gave way to a locked jaw.

Woman: "Oh."

And she walked away.

Why was the wind knocked out of this woman's proverbial sails? Why did she walk away dejected? If she were in touch
with a real love and compassion for Tim and if she simultaneously believed that knowing Christ was the ultimate good, then
wouldn't she naturally be joyful—and maybe even exhibit a
curiosity about what God was doing in Tim's life?

"Let the Word of Christ dwell in you richly…" (Colossians 3:16 NIV). "Dwelling richly" seems to have a connotation
that extends beyond mere opinions about God. It seems to transcend passing along information about God. And it seems like
something much more exciting and purposeful than just sharing
the Good News because it's our duty.

In John 15, Jesus speaks of the necessity of remaining
or abiding in Him, which inevitably will produce fruit. It is a
simple science really. It's a matter of internalizing the Gospel,
then expressing the truth of the Word out of our own experience
and interaction with Christ. John is told to eat it, making it part
of him—becoming what he is about to say. We, too, are called to
speak out of what is real—not just theologically, but experien-
tially.

"Taste and see that the Lord is good."

(Psalm 34:8 NIV)

There is another truth in these verses about how people
receive the Gospel. In John's mouth, the words were sweet, but
in his stomach, the words were as nasty as the expired yogurt I
once ate. In other words, in spite of (or perhaps even, in light of)
our alignment with God's heart for people and our honest desire
for them to taste His good grace, the Good News isn't always
received as good. There is a part of the Gospel that is sweet and
pleasant but there is another side that is costly and difficult.
The cost of discipleship—denying the pull of sin and self-cen-

31

teredness in order to repent and carry the cross of Christ—isn't so palatable. In fact, the notion of dying to one's self in order to live for Christ is offensive to one's Ptolemaic notion that the world revolves around them. Often the Gospel is rejected and, as witnesses, we can experience the bitterness of that rejection.

Last night I was talking to Bob and Maddie, friends from the neighborhood, who were lamenting that our mutual neighbors are moving away to another country. We agreed that it is bittersweet. We are truly excited for them and the next chapter of their lives, but we will miss their friendship.

Bob and Maddie are believers and are both saddened and frustrated that for the three years they've known them, our neighbors-on-the-move have been totally resistant to anything related to Christianity.

Maddie acknowledged that she and Bob had tried to love them well and to honestly share their lives but felt that if she had pressed the conversation about God or faith any further, the door would have been completely shut. She's probably right.

A person's negative response, whether apathy or animosity, can and should break our hearts, but it does not diminish the reality of the Gospel, nor does it diminish the validity of our own storyline. It does, however, reiterate the role of the witness.

Converting people is not our job. It's God's job. God, in His sovereignty, has chosen to love humanity in such a way that it can choose whether or not to love Him back. In our attempt to mimic the way of Jesus' love, our job has often been compared to what D.T. Niles referred to as "one beggar telling another beggar where he found bread."[1] (Check out the beggars sharing bread story in 1 Kings 7.) We have the important role of telling people where we find Life, but we are not the givers of life.

A TRUTHFUL WITNESS

When we encounter the grace and goodness of God, any hint of the disingenuous dissipates. Grace compels us to live truthfully, with personal integrity. Being a witness means we refuse to put on masks of pretense. The Good News isn't that we have it all together, that we have it all figured out. The Good News is that in our brokenness, God keeps putting us back together. He keeps restoring shalom.

Paul wrote the words, "It's for freedom that Christ has set us free" (Galatians 5:1 NIV). We are free to be honest with our lives. The hiding of our true selves (our struggles, our past, our messiness) keeps the Gospel on the top shelf, out of reach. You and I being the redeemed-but-honestly-still-in-process-and-reliant-on-His-grace-version of ourselves is the best witness to the life-giving reality of Jesus. An honest witness further validates the power and potency of the Gospel. Paul encouraged Timothy, "Set an example for the believers in speech, in life, in love, in faith, and in purity" (1 Timothy 4:12 NIV). We must narrow the chasm between what we say and what we do. "This is the reality of my life and, frankly, I can't shut up about it."

Like newly engaged couples telling everyone who will stop to listen, it's hard to keep this kind of news quiet. What a contrast to the guilt-ridden, fear-laden, joyless duty of compartmentalizing evangelism into something we begrudgingly do.

When we are captured by the grace of Jesus, when the message of the cross and empty tomb are internalized, the Gospel isn't something that is simply shared—the Gospel is passionately lived. This is Christ in us, transforming us by His grace, His light shining through us.

"God made my life complete
when I placed all the pieces before him
When I got my act together,
he gave me a fresh start.
Now I am alert to God's ways;
I don't take God for granted
Every day I review the ways he works;
I try not to miss a trick
I feel put back together,
and I'm watching my step.
God rewrote the text of my life
when I opened the book of my heart to his eyes."
(Psalms 18:20–24 MSG)

You are a witness. You have seen; you have heard; you have tasted this Good News, this Gospel.

CONSIDER THIS
Witness Redefined

1. Has "being a witness" to something ever cost you anything?

2. When was a time you should have spoken up but instead were silent? When was a time you should have remained silent but instead spoke up?

3. How do you live out the tension between the humility and ownership that comes with being a witness? Do you lean toward one side or the other? Do you struggle with one side or the other?

4. Do you use your lack of knowledge as an excuse to refuse the responsibility of being a witness?

5. "The grace and truth of Jesus must become a part of you before you speak about them. This is the essence of witness." How has the grace and truth of Jesus become a part of you?

6. "The hiding of our true selves [our struggles, our past, our messiness] keeps the Gospel on the top shelf, out of reach." Why are we tempted to mask our real selves?

7. How does the reality of God's grace and unconditional love free us from our masks?

8. How have you seen, heard, and tasted the Good News of the Gospel?

1. Niles, D.T.. *That They May Have Life*. New York: Harpers and Brothers ,1951.

YOU ARE A
WITNESS.
YOU HAVE SEEN;
YOU HAVE HEARD;
YOU HAVE TASTED
THIS GOOD NEWS,
THIS GOSPEL.

chapter Three

The Pull
of the Gospel

[Our Motivation in Coming Alongside]

Telemarketer [in telemarketer voice]: "Is this Robert Scrumpppfff?"

Me: "Close enough."

Telemarketer: "Mr. Scrumpppfff, I have some very good news for you this evening. I'm calling to let you know that you've been selected to receive a free three-day, two-night stay in lovely Branson, Missouri."

Me: "No, thanks."

Telemarketer: "I'm sorry. What was that?"

Me: "No."

Telemarketer: "Excuse me?"

Me: "No, thank you. I have no desire whatsoever to go to Branson."

Telemarketer: (complete silence)

Me: "In fact, I would rather have bamboo shoots shoved under my fingernails than to endure the mayhem of that town."

Telemarketer: (laughs and responds in non-telemarketer voice) "Shoot, I hear you, man! They couldn't pay me to go to Branson either!"

You may have heard the old adage, "Are you smoking what you're selling?" This query is designed to cut to the heart of personal integrity. Is your life aligned with what you advertise? The same question is relevant to us as witnesses.

When it comes to the Gospel, do we actually believe it is Good News? Have we experienced it? Have we internalized it? Why is the Gospel good? How do we know? Who is this Good News for? Before you tell it or live it, you have to believe it. Or, as Tim Keller says, "We have to recapture the essence of the Gospel, but the Gospel has to recapture us."

GOSPEL

In Greek, the word for Gospel is εὐαγγέλιον, which is defined as "good news." It is where we English speakers derive the word "evangelism."

Contrary to popular belief, evangelism isn't confined to Christianity. I read that Google has a "Chief Internet Evangelist," as does Apple. Apple's guy defines evangelism as "selling your dream so that other people believe in it as much as you do."

For the Jesus follower, it's not about selling a rapidly outdated dream; it's about sharing and expressing one's hope, faith, love, and vision of restoration that is anchored in the transcendent depths of God's good grace. It's about sharing one's story because that story is wrapped around His Story, the Gospel. Our lives are compilations of stories of where we came from, where we are, where we're going, what we think, and what we believe. All of these components work together to make us who we are.

Toben Heim wrote, "At our core, we are walking anthologies made up of the stories of our experiences."[1]

The good news is that God pulls us into His big Story, a three-act play with an eternity's worth of curtain calls:

Act 1: Good news. God creates out of and for relationship.

Act 2: Bad news. Sin disconnects and destroys that intimacy.

Act 3: Good News. God redeems the story and restores the brokenness.

GOD'S STORY ENGAGES WITH THE BIG QUESTIONS

Who am I? Where did I come from? Where do I belong? What is the purpose of my life? When we encounter His Story we get changed—not just our behavior, but our attitudes and motivation. Our will is challenged. We become unstuck from our perpetual self-centeredness. Our engagement with His Story is one in which we are called to respond, to embrace the reality of the cross and the resurrection, the reality of Jesus.

If we are leveled by the reality of God's Story, we move from "have to" to "want to" to "can't not."

HAVE TO

This is the essence of religious duty. It is infused with the toxic veneer of legalism that has an appearance of righteousness and an illusion of intimacy, but whose actual ingredients are guilt and fear.

The posture of "have to" is minimalistic and calculated. It desires clear-cut requirements in order to do the bare minimum and precludes any notion of grace or trust that is essential for relationship, as explained in this verse:

"These people honor me with their lips but their hearts are far from me."
(Matthew 15:8 NIV)

WANT TO

This is the essence of the gift of grace. The backdrop of "want to" is the wide-open space of freedom and trust. It flows out of an honest process, not a task list. It is a place where our desires are aligned with His desires. This is precluded by trust that grows out of knowing God, not just knowing about Him. This knowing most likely stems from honest wrestling and questioning—always in proximity to Him, always aware of His love.

A.W. Tozer wrote, "Thirsty hearts are those whose longings have been awakened by the touch of God within them."[2] We are simply responding to the work He has done and is doing in us, because we want to.

CAN'T NOT

This is the essence of passion, allowing God's grace and truth to change us so that we can't help but care and act from His perspective. The terrain of "can't not" is rugged and at times ambiguous. There is a sustainability that extends beyond the emotion of the altar call but also stays pliable, moldable, and teachable. It is a confident humility—humbled by grace, confident in truth. It is a willingness to follow and live for Christ and let Him dictate the terms of that discipleship. It is the point of relinquishment of self. We can't not respond.

> **"But if I say, 'I will not mention him or speak any more in his name,' his word is in my heart like a fire, a fire shut up in my bones. I am weary of holding it in; indeed, I cannot."**
> *(Jeremiah 20:9 NIV)*

Sure, when you were growing up, your mother forced you to hug your great aunt even though she smelled like mothballs and garlic. You technically had to because if you didn't, your mother would ground you for life—but that was a bit of an exception.

In reality, no one is forcing you to love God or to love people. In fact, the nature of love is that God created us with the capacity to accept or reject His love and He created us with the capacity to reciprocate or withhold our love of Him and humanity.

So, on the one hand, you "ain't got to."

But when you realize how much God loves you and to what extent He has gone to pursue and rescue you, and when you actually allow yourself to be loved by Him, then "you ain't got to" (love Him back), but you can't help it. And when the light bulb switches on, when you start to realize what God thinks about this world and what violence, poverty, and injustice do to His heart . . .

When you start to view the mass of humanity through His lens, which has the capacity to see each unique individual, created in His image, for the purpose of bringing glory to His name . . .

When you see the shadow of the cross fall on the whole world and not just in your backyard . . .

When you start to realize the depth and the cost of God's love for every man, woman, and child . . .

Then you "ain't got to" (love that world or those people), but you can't help it.

Every day we come into contact with a world and with individuals within that world who have no idea about this Good News. We have the privilege of helping them connect the dots. We are not inviting them to a building or a program or to an investment in fire insurance. We are inviting them to a Person. We are extending an invitation to Reality and this Reality, this Jesus, changes us from the inside out—an inner transformation that spills out into the streets and cubicles and corners of society and culture.

EITHER/OR

On the one hand, the presentation of the Gospel has been very much about the individual. In the last century, the message of evangelistic programs, events, and resources has been focused on the personal.

- "You can have a personal relationship with Christ."
- "If you were the only person on earth, Jesus still would have died on the cross to save you."
- "If you were to die tonight, do you know where you would spend eternity?"
- "All you have to do is pray this prayer; then you can spend eternity in heaven."

The approach to teaching methods of evangelism has been focused on the individual, as well.

- "Learn how to share your personal testimony."
- "You are the only Bible some people ever read."

There has been a built-in pressure to perform or to look like you have it all together because you "don't know who's watching you, and you need to be a good witness."

On the other hand, over the past few years there has been a shift regarding the nature of Christianity in general, and subsequently regarding evangelism as well, with more emphasis on the Kingdom of God and community. In accordance with this focus comes the ever-true but freshly recognized reality, that yes, Jesus came to save you, but He also came to save the other billions besides you.

The Biblical narrative has been expanded beyond a focus on The Fall and atonement to include the Genesis mandate as outlined in Genesis 1:26-28 and 2:15. This "cultural mandate" is a call to be creative and thoughtful stewards of what God has made, to care for creation and live in the reality of the coming promise of restoration—not of just our lives (if we are in Christ), but the whole of humanity and creation. There has been a renewal of Jesus' message that the Kingdom of God is here and now.

As things often go in the church, it has seemed like an either/or—pick-your-side-of-the-fence debate over the nature of the Gospel. But I believe Jesus is calling us to something else.

BOTH/AND

A personal relationship with God is vital but there are very public ramifications to such a relationship. Learning how to share your personal story of how He has changed your life is important, but it's not the whole picture; just like the arching themes of justice and a "Kingdom of God" mentality are important, but not the whole picture. It's the entire view that matters most.

The Gospel Story is one of both personal salvation and the restoration of all things, of individual transformation and cultural revolution. It affects not only our eternal status, but what we do with the rest of our lives in the meantime.

The claim of the Gospel is that it puts us in touch with reality—all of it, not just a part. It puts us in touch with a God who creates and with people and world He created. It puts us in touch with a Christ who redeems and the people whom He loves. It puts us in touch with our feelings of hope and despair, with our thoughts of doubt and faith, with our acts of virtue and vice. It puts us in touch with everything visible and invisible, right and wrong, good and evil. We live in a world where people are going crazy. We have a gospel that sets us free to think, and in so doing it develops us in a rich and robust sanity. The sanity of the gospel is one of its most attractive features. Persons who truly live by faith are in touch with reality and become conspicuously sane.[3]

(Eugene Peterson, *Living The Message*)

The Gospel is incredibly honest about why the world is so chaotic, in a big picture sort of way. It does not give the particulars about God's mind and will, but does give us a context for understanding our loneliness, our susceptibility to sin, and our dissatisfaction with the way things are. It does not ignore the darkness of injustice and poverty, addiction and brokenness. On the contrary, it shines the purest form of light on them— light that not only exposes the vulgarity, but brings the hope of truth and grace.

- The Gospel doesn't gloss over the past and the things we have done or things done to us, but it does rescue us from the cramped cell of suppression into the vast freedom of what it means to be known and loved and accepted in the deepest way.

- The Gospel brings us out of the anxiety-ridden assumption that God loves us if—if we get our crap together, if we behave, if we do enough good things to offset the bad things— and into the whispered confidence that God loves us, not "if," but "because." Because He is love.

- The Gospel message isn't that God tolerates you; it's that He loves you.

- The Gospel has at its root the death, burial, and resurrection of Jesus. Its branches are the fruitfulness of the community of believers, lived out in a world that is hungry for that fruit.

- The Gospel shows up in the most surprising of places and

changes people forever. It tells us that we are known. We are loved. We have worth and meaning.

- The Gospel gives us a deep confidence, trust, and peace that enables us to actually see and care about what is going on around us in order to love and serve others.

- The Gospel is news that is too good to keep to ourselves. It must be lived. It must be told. It must be expressed in every fiber of our being.

My wife Lea has described this "both/and" approach to the Gospel this way: "The closer I get to God, the more I realize my need for Him. And the more I realize my need for Him, the more I can spot that need in others, as well. That's why He calls us to love one another. The more I walk along beside people for the long-haul and love them, the more sharing Christ becomes reflexive because in my heart I'm convinced that He is the only one who can truly heal and satisfy."

Good news isn't to be hoarded. It is to be shared. Jesus said it would be foolish to light a candle and hide it. Likewise, evangelism is an overflow of belief—belief that God is Who He says He is. That He's done what He says He's done. That He will do what He has promised He'll do. And because of that, your story and my story have been redeemed and rewritten with a new ending and it is good.

Until we truly believe His Story, evangelism will simply continue to be something we reluctantly do, and cease to be the essence of who we are.

There are a plethora of motivations for sharing one's faith, such as guilt, a desire for some sort of bonus points, a sense of duty, or even for bragging rights. However, there is only one motivation that actually compels us with integrity, passion, and sustainability.

"For Christ's love compels us, because we are convinced that one died for all, and therefore all died. And he died for all, that those who live should no longer live for themselves, but for him who died for them and was raised again."

(2 Corinthians 5:14–15 NIV)

It's when we are leveled by the cross, when we let Him change our story with His, that we begin to allow His Spirit to take our eyes off of ourselves in order to see and love the world around us. That's the motivation; that's the pull.

In a word, grace.

When we receive and experience this Good News and can get past our assumptions, cynicism, and self-centeredness and allow ourselves to breathe it in, to embrace it, and to be leveled by the grace of God, then the Gospel of the Kingdom of Jesus Christ will become our passion, our thought, our decision, our compulsion, and our life.

"For we know, brothers loved by God, that he has chosen you, because our gospel came to you not simply with words, but also with power, with the Holy Spirit and with deep conviction."

(1 Thessalonians 1:4–5 NIV)

Be the Gospel so others will embrace the Gospel; so they will get in on this thing called grace.

CONSIDER THIS
The Pull of The Gospel

1. In what areas of your life and faith do you live in the reality of "have to?" What areas do you live in "want to?" What areas do you live in "can't not?"

2. If applicable, what compelled your transformation from "have to" to "want to" to "can't not"?

3. Evangelism is the overflow of belief. What parts of the reality of the Gospel are more difficult for you to truly believe?

4. What really motivates you to share your faith?

5. "The closer I get to God, the more I realize my need for Him. And the more I realize my need for Him, the more I can spot that need in others, as well." How has this reality played out in your life?

6. Are you in touch with your need for God? In what area, relationship, or situation in your life are you most in need of God? What needs do you see around you that can only truly be healed and satisfied by God? What is your response to that?

1. Heim, Toben. The Simple Wife. www.hesimplewife.typepad.com.
2. Tozer, A.W..The Pursuit of God. Harrisburg, PA: Christian Publications, 1948.2.
3. Peterson, Eugene. Living The Mesaage. New York: HarperOne Publishing, 2007.

BE THE GOSPEL
SO OTHERS WILL
EMBRACE THE
GOSPEL; SO THEY
WILL GET IN ON
THIS THING CALLED
GRACE.

Chapter Four

Concentric Circles of Grace

[Receiving and Extending Grace
in the Midst of the Grey]

We experience grace in a lot of different ways: Realizing we overpaid our taxes on the same day we receive a huge bill. A cool rain on a scorching August afternoon. The sun's rays peeking through the dimly painted sky in the midst of a long winter. A stranger in the next lane waving us over when we have ignored the "Merge Left" sign for half a mile. A friend refusing the urge to tell us, "I told you so." Valuable friends reminding us of who we are and the possibilities for our lives, despite our failures and immaturity.

I was brought up hearing about grace and even seeing it demonstrated in the lives of people around me. But for me, personally, the concept of grace was more of an elusive theological premise than a known reality until I was twenty-one years old.

I kept myself perpetually busy with Christian things, wearing a kind of mask that pretended to have it all together, unaware of the true need I had for this Jesus whom I had been studying about in Bible College.

One night, God's goodness and love became a reality in my life. I was alone in a dark, musty old chapel pouring my heart out to God via the out-of-tune piano. I became acutely aware that in the midst of my busyness, there was a dissatisfaction with the way things were going. I didn't hear an audible voice or have a light flood the space, but I definitely "heard" God's Spirit asking the questions, "Why are you doing what you're doing? What is driving the achievement, the perpetual motion, the titles, and the grades? Are you aware of how much you need me? Are you aware of how much I love you?"

It was the first time I think I really started to understand my need for grace. Simultaneously I found that I wanted it desperately but was reluctant to reach out and receive it, for fear of shattering the illusion that I was the one calling the shots. If I were going to truly accept the sufficiency of God's grace, I would have to finally admit my need for a Savior and let go of achievement-driven religion.

A few years ago, U2 wrote a song about this, appropriately entitled "Grace."[1] There are several great lyrics in the song, but the line, "She travels outside of karma," has always stood out to me. Karma is "the cause and effect action of bringing upon yourself inevitable results"—of earning good things for your life by being a good person. The theory of karma is prevalent in Buddhism and Hinduism, and though the concept is counter to the message of the Gospel, too often in Christianity we have karma in disguise. Karma says we're basically good people so we deserve good things. We deserve salvation. We deserve God's blessing. We deserve things to work out well for us.

Grace, on the other hand, says we could never be "good enough," so instead of trying to earn salvation and blessing, we are simply to receive them.

The interesting thing about grace is that it has a habit of breaking cycles of sin, but also breaking cycles of self-righteousness.

Grace not only saves us, it's what allows us to live. "All over the world this Gospel is bearing fruit and growing, just as it has been doing among you since the day you heard it and understood God's grace in all its truth" (Colossians 1:6 NIV).

If our motivation in this life is a response to His love, then there is no room for ego or self-reliance. An understanding of grace requires us to stay connected to and dependent upon God. We not only recognize the world's need for Jesus, we recognize our need for Him every moment. Legalism and entitlement need God only occasionally for an endorsement or to get out of a jam. Living in grace is the acknowledgement of our total dependence. Why would we presume to achieve grace?

Grace does not give us a license to sin, nor does it demand we keep sin hidden in order to maintain the appearance of external piety. Grace exposes us in our brokenness, but then frees us to let the righteousness of Christ become our identity, our motivation, and our purpose in life. We are saved "from" sin but also "for" righteousness.

To paraphrase Paul, "Why in the world would we flirt around with sin?" Why would we opt for the anxiety of sin management over the freedom of Christ's atonement? Why would we compare our sin to that of others in order to minimize or justify our decisions? Why would we live under the illusion that we can indulge the flesh while we simultaneously attempt to walk in the Spirit?

We must take sin seriously, not in order to produce guilt or piety, but in order to more fully understand and live out grace. We must be a community of believers that acknowledges its brokenness and suspends judgment, but also a community that refuses to enable one another to stay stuck in the muck of our sin. We must model what it means to confess sin and to let the ongoing cleansing of Christ keep us free from being entangled by it.

Grace changes us in a way that motivates us to extend it to others.

Grace never ends up in a cul-de-sac of piety or self-centeredness.

We receive grace in its various forms.

We extend grace in its various forms.

We breathe in grace.

We breathe out grace.

We are consumed by His grace and truth in a way that transforms our thinking and attitude, motivation and heart, as we are changed by the indwelling presence of Jesus. But in the process of living in that reality, we start to realize that it's not really about us. It's about Him and we start to pay attention to what He is up to.

HOW DOES HE FEEL ABOUT THE WORLD HE CAME TO SAVE?

How does He feel specifically about the person down the hall or down the street whom you see every day? How does He feel about your friends, your co-workers or fellow students, and your time?

HOW DOES HE FEEL ABOUT YOU?

Grace is a gift. It comes in a thousand forms, give or take whatever number Peter implies by his use of the word "various." It is meant to be received in its various forms and it is meant to be dispensed in its various forms (1 Peter 4:10).

Grace makes a huge splash, but the waves it creates go way beyond the baptism pool because God's love has a ripple effect—concentric circles of grace.

Here is one such story about concentric circles from the Old Testament.

The King of Aram desperately wanted to attack Israel, but Elisha the prophet kept giving intel to Israel's king about how to avoid the attacks which, as you can imagine, made the King of Aram increasingly agitated.

At first, the King of Aram thought there must be a double agent who was leaking information, but then he was told about Elisha the prophet and his annoying habit of telling Israel's king all the thoughts and plans of Aram's king. Because of this, Aram's King decided to get rid of Elisha, so he sent a huge army to the city of Dothan where Elisha was living. During the night, they completely surrounded the city, and in the morning when Elisha's young apprentice went out to fetch some water to cook breakfast, he completely lost his appetite (and most likely the previous day's lunch) when he saw that they were surrounded by the enemy of Israel—complete with horses, chariots, and mean guys with weapons.

"Oh my lord, what shall we do?"

Elisha's reaction was very Obi-Wan-ish. (Insert British accent for effect.) "Don't be afraid. Those who are with us are more than those who are with them."

As Elisha's servant is recalculating the numbers and questioning the math skills of the seemingly insane prophet man, Elisha started praying.

"O Lord, open his eyes so he may see."

Then the Lord opened the servant's eyes, and he looked and saw the hills covered with horses and chariots of fire all around Elisha—the army of God.

As the enemy closes in, Elisha prayed to the Lord, "Strike these people with blindness," which God did, and then the Bible tells us Elisha led the sightless army to the capital of Israel where he insisted that the King extend them grace. And instead of killing the army of Aram, the Israelites threw a big party for the them (2 Kings 6.)

It is a very cool story about God's power, God's grace, and God's sovereignty. It's also a story about concentric circles.

Elisha's servant boy doesn't have a name. We'll call him Sam. All Sam could see was the ring of animosity, the threat to his wellbeing, to his schedule, to his plans, and to his very life. These were insurmountable odds—two men against hundreds of well-armed soldiers riding on chariots. He had seen or at least heard of God doing some interesting things as of late—providing for a widow, curing a guy of leprosy, having bears maul some juvenile delinquents who had made fun of Elisha—but this was different.

This appears to be the end: the end of Sam's promising career, the end of his ideas, the end of his life. We know the feeling.

- We look up and all we can see is that we are hemmed in by our circumstances.
- We feel entrapped by the cycles of sin or the power of addiction.
- We feel overwhelmed by fear that we are not good enough—that we will never be good enough.
- We feel paralyzed by the fear of making the wrong choice.
- We feel we are breaking under the weight of the law—trying to follow all the rules, and trying to do it perfectly.

Jesus said, "In this world you will have trouble." He knew that inevitably we would be surrounded by all sorts of things that bring doubt, questions, stress, fear, and (potentially) apathy. He knew that we would be perpetually overwhelmed and exhausted from dealing with the brokenness. But into this, Jesus said something very peculiar.

"Cheer up. I have overcome the world."
(John 16:33)

The Greek word is tharseo, which means "be of good courage." There is another circle, another ring.

Elisha prayed for his servant to have a new prescription to see farther, to see beyond—to see the ring of God's presence, provision, and power encircling and thus dismantling the ring of fear, despair, and impending doom that dominated his field of vision.

"God is our refuge and strength, an ever-present help in trouble. Therefore we will not fear, though the earth give way and the mountains fall into the heart of the sea, though its waters roar and foam and the mountains quake with their surging. Be still and know that I am God."

(Psalms 46:1–3, 10 NIV)

Interestingly, grace shows up most vividly when we get to the end of ourselves, when we are completely spent, when our vision is blurred.

GRACE SHOWS UP IN THE GREY.

"Are you tired? Worn out? Burned out on religion? Come to me. Get away with me and you'll recover your life. I'll show you how to take a real rest. Walk with me and work with me—watch how I do it. Learn the unforced rhythms of grace. I won't lay anything heavy or ill-fitting on you. Keep company with me and you'll learn to live freely and lightly."

(Matthew 11:28–30 MSG)

BREATHE GRACE IN. BREATHE GRACE OUT.

"Praise be to the God and Father of our Lord Jesus Christ, the Father of compassion and the God of all comfort, who comforts us in all our troubles, so that we can comfort those in any trouble with the comfort we ourselves have received from God."

(2 Corinthians 1:3 NIV)

Because we have been forgiven, we forgive. Because we have been comforted with a peace that goes beyond understanding, we comfort others. Because we have experienced God's grace, we feel the confidence and freedom to share this Kingdom mentality with others without fear or pretense.

And that takes us back to this:

"But you will receive power when the Holy Spirit comes on you; and you will be my witnesses in Jerusalem, and in all Judea and Samaria, and to the ends of the earth."

(Acts 1:8 NIV)

Jesus stated that, collectively, our stories have a ripple effect that travel in concentric circles to the ends of the earth and affect the "now" as well as the "not yet," both present and eternal reality: "You will be my witnesses in Jerusalem, Judea and Samaria, and to the ends of the earth." Both spiritually and geographically, we tell the Story from wherever we are, on whatever page.

As you go, make disciples. Come alongside people with the desire to help them align with the grace and truth of Jesus. As you go to class, as you go to work, as you order a cup of coffee, as you play ultimate frisbee, as you confront life and love neighbors; as you go, you get to be what Paul calls an "ambassador of reconciliation."

• You get to serve people in the most random and the most deliberate of ways.

• You get to love people who are hard to love and learn something from them.

• You get to listen, to discern, and to creatively extend grace in a thousand forms.

• You get to paint the picture of grace from your unique vantage point.

We receive grace in its various forms. Grace that overwhelms whatever is overwhelming us.

We extend grace in its various forms. Grace that brings wholeness and healing and hope.

We breathe in grace.

We breathe out grace.

One more concentric circle.

THE LIGHT OF THE WORLD

In John 8, Jesus says, "I am the light of the world." In Matthew 5, Jesus says, "You are the light of the world." Which is it? Is Jesus the light or are we the light?

Yes. Sort of.

"Jesus spoke to the people once more and said, 'I am the light of the world. If you follow me, you won't have to walk in darkness, because you will have the light that leads to life.'"

(John 8:12 NLT)

"For God, who said, 'Let light shine out of darkness,' made his light shine in our hearts to give us the light of the knowledge of the glory of God in the face of Christ."

(2 Corinthians 4:6 NIV)

IT'S ALL ABOUT HIM. HE IS THE LIGHT.

When we are in close proximity to Him, then we reflect that light. We reflect Jesus.

"For you were once darkness, but now you are light in the Lord. Live as children of light . . . "

(Ephesians 5:8 NIV)

"He called you out of the darkness into his wonderful light."

(1 Peter 2:9 NLT)

"You are the light of the world. Like a city on a hilltop that cannot be hidden."

(Matthew 5:14 NLT)

"This is the message we heard from Jesus and now declare to you: God is light, and there is no darkness in him at all. So we are lying if we say we have fellowship with God but go on living in spiritual darkness; we are not practicing the truth. But if we are living in the light, as God is in the light, then we have fellowship with each other, and the blood of Jesus, his Son, cleanses us from all sin."

(1 John 1:5–7 NLT)

That is the whole idea of being a follower of Jesus. Not to see how far away from the light we can get and still be "technically" visible. Not to stay in the shadows so we can have one foot in the darkness and one foot in the light.

Being a follower of Jesus means to stay close to Him, and in staying close to Jesus, we inevitably stay close to one another. And we start to pick up on the way He thinks, what He does, and the kind of people He hangs out with. We get a sense of His heart for the broken and the oppressed, and we become aware of what He thinks is important. In the process, we become a part of something distinctive—like a city on a hill at night glowing with something that is real because Jesus is reality and Paul says we have been given the fullness of Jesus. John also wrote:

"For of His fullness we have all received, and grace upon grace."

(John 1:16 NASB)

GRACE UPON GRACE

Many of you have experienced, or are experiencing, or are hopefully about to experience the grace of God in real and tangible ways. Each of you could tell stories about what God has done or express what you might be sensing He is about to do in your life. Many of you could share your own Elisha's servant-type stories of feeling completely surrounded by sin or addictions, past abuse or depression, legalistic baggage or fear. My prayer is that even as you read this, the nearsightedness of the problem is starting to give way to the bigger picture of God's provision, His protection, His forgiveness, and His intense love for you. My prayer is that the restored version of your story becomes an impetus for someone else to be curious about this Jesus.

Many of you can sense something new stirring in your life—a desire to share with others what God has been doing in you—to love people, to serve people, to help others get in on God's good grace.

Grace received in a thousand stories.

Grace extended in a thousand forms.

Grace extended to you and me in order to be re-extended to a world desperate for it.

CONSIDER THIS
Concentric Circles of Grace

1. What are some ways you have personally experienced the grace of God?

2. Have you ever had a difficult time receiving God's grace or believing that He could actually love you?

3. What circumstances or fears have "encircled" you in the past? Presently?

4. Can you pray for your eyes to be opened to the reality of God overwhelming whatever is overwhelming you?

5. "Both spiritually and geographically, we tell the Story from wherever we are, on whatever page." On what page are you, geographically?

6. Who is in your unique sphere of influence?

7. What specific situation or setting has God placed you in right now?

8. Where are you spiritually? What has God been up to in your story recently?

9. What would it look like to reflect the light of Christ to your friends, family, neighbors, co-workers, etc.?

1. Bono. "Grace." All That You Can't Leave Behind. Island Records, 2000.

GRACE RECEIVED
IN A THOUSAND
STORIES.
GRACE EXTENDED
IN A THOUSAND
FORMS.

Chapter Five

Grace by Proxy

[Discipleship as the Essence of Coming Alongside]

"One day as Jesus was walking along the shore of the Sea of Galilee, he saw two brothers—Simon, also called Peter, and Andrew—throwing a net into the water, for they fished for a living. Jesus called out to them, 'Come, follow me, and I will show you how to fish for people!' And they left their nets at once and followed him."

(Matthew 4:18–20 NLT)

They dropped their nets to follow Jesus. What an unexpected honor it was in that culture to be called by a rabbi to follow and become a disciple, a learner, and an apprentice. As a Jewish male, it was the best thing one could hope for, and it would have been a special privilege for these men because the fact that they were fishing for a living probably meant they had already flunked out of rabbi school. They were, no doubt, perplexed and excited about Jesus' invitation.

Jesus was inviting them to come alongside Him as He came alongside humanity.

To watch as He touched lepers and healed their bodies.

To listen as He taught with authority.

To ask questions when they didn't get it.

To feel compassion the way Jesus felt compassion.

To be changed.

To become like Jesus by being with Jesus.

In the same way Jesus called an eclectic group of men to follow Him with their lives, so He calls us. Our own journey has a different geography and topography, but it bears the same destination. It is a journey to the cross. Beyond self-awareness, it is a call to the relinquishment of self, a relationship with Jesus that completely transforms every aspect of our lives. It is an invitation to trust Him with everything, to love and be loved.

Each day looks different, but it is a journey closer in both proximity and understanding to Jesus. In following Him, we are inevitably drawn closer to knowing ourselves, each other, and the world around us. Jesus doesn't impose His way on us—He invites. Or as Eugene Peterson says, "He shows us the way. He is the way—more than a road, a line on a map that we can use to find our way to eternal life. The Way that is Jesus cannot be reduced to information or instruction. The way is a person whom we believe and follow."[1]

THE PROCESS OF THAT FOLLOWING—OF THIS JOURNEY—IS CALLED DISCIPLE-SHIP.

A lot of what I heard at church growing up was that the Christian life was all about getting someone saved. Getting people to move from lost to found, from darkness to light, to say "the prayer," and to be baptized. That was the destination. Sinner is saved. Angels throw a party. Church grows.

Don't get me wrong, conversion is a big deal. But conversion is not the destination of this journey.

Think about a wedding day.

It's the big day. The bride has been dreaming of this day since she was a little girl and now it is here, and everything is perfect. The chapel is filled with friends and family. The music has begun and the bridal party is in place. Her father walks her down the aisle to greet her soon-to-be husband. Vows are made, rings exchanged, the pronouncement declared, and the bride and groom make their exit to a sea of bubbles, load into the limo, and make their way to the reception where they have the biggest celebration anyone has ever seen. There is the first dance, the cutting of the cake, and the throwing of the garter where all the single men in the crowd pretend to care. Then comes the throwing of the bouquet where the single women in the crowd pretend to not care—until it's airborne. Pictures are taken. Food is consumed. Champaign-filled glasses are raised in toasts. It's quite the wedding.

As the bride grabs the microphone, the music and conversation hush and everyone leans in to hear what she will say about her new marriage. "Thank you so much for coming and thank you, Ross, for being such a great fiancé these past eight years. Today was everything I had always dreamed it would be. It was beautiful. It was fun. Ross, I sincerely hope you have a nice life and someday meet the woman of your dreams. You deserve it. Good night everybody." Then she hops in the limo and makes her exit.

That would be a curious thing, n'est-ce pas?

The wedding ceremony is obviously not the end of the journey. The point of a wedding is to mark the beginning of a marriage where two people are devoted to the ongoing deepening of the relationship. The point of conversion is not simply the conversion, it anticipates ongoing relational discipleship and intentionally living for the glory of Christ.

Jesus wants to lead people out from this overgrown thicket of self-destruction and sinful delusion into the openness of His grace and life; but the journey doesn't stop there. He wants us to keep walking with Him. A disciple is a learner, an understudy, someone who pays close attention and tries to imitate. A disciple of Jesus is a person who spends time serving, listening, and talking to Him, but also spends time serving, listening, and talking to those who have yet to meet Him and know His good grace.

YOU ARE SENT

Jesus said, "As the Father has sent Me, I am sending you."
(John 20:21 NIV)

Writer Jason Zahariades says that we are "God's sent people."[2] Wherever followers of Christ are, that's where church is. So how are we being church where we are?

I don't pose this question as a guilt trip; just as a reality check. Being the church is having an awareness of the reality of who we are in Christ, a group of Jesus' apprentices who are learning how to be sent.

I believe God is sending us corporately (and many of us individually) to make disciples in other parts of the world as we carry out both the Matthew 25 part of the Great Commission of feeding the hungry, clothing the sick, caring for the imprisoned; and the James chapter 1 part of the Great Commission, which calls us to "[care] for the orphans and widows." But I believe sometimes we overlook the "as you go" part of the Great Commission (see Matthew 28).

After a trip to Biloxi, Mississippi, following Hurricane Katrina a few years ago, one of our students said what many of us know to be true. "It was such an easy decision to go to the Gulf Coast, yet it's so hard to go across the hall." The Great Commission has local implications as much as global implications.

Jesus' commission begins with the words, "As you go, make disciples." As we go, there are some specific roles to fill.

CONNECT

Acts 17 is a snapshot of what it means to connect the dots. Paul was in the city of Athens having a conversation with people who had various world-views. Back then, Philosophy wasn't a side item or a two-hour credit you took at the university; it was a way of life. In his words to the Athenians (of which we have only a snapshot, as this most likely was a conversation over a number of days), Paul affirmed the Athenians' spiritual interest and search for truth.

He quoted their poets. He approached them philosophically and challenged the way they were trying to satisfy the hunger of their souls. Paul gave them surprising evidence that supported his message and pointed to an unexpected way to fulfill their spiritual search—through Jesus. I think it is important that, although respectful and thoughtful, Paul doesn't back down from the reality of the resurrection. In fact, that's what ended the discussion and for some it was too much and they dismissed him and his words as just another fad. But others were curious, not just about this Jesus, but about the way this Jew was talking about Him.

In a sentence, Paul was unapologetic in his careful and compassionate apologetic.

APOLOGETIC VS. APOLOGETIC

Apologetic: giving caveats for inconveniencing people with the most incredible news that they've ever heard. Namely that Jesus died so they can live, that through Him they can experience freedom, and that He loves them as they are.

Versus . . .

Apologetic: thinking and wrestling through what we believe so that we can, in the words of Simon Peter, "give the story for the hope that is in us" in a way that makes sense. It means to provide reasonable answers to honest questions and to do so with humility, respect, and reverence. "Let your conversation be always full of grace, seasoned with salt, so that you may know how to answer everyone" (Colossians 4:6 NIV).

'Taking a stand' today rarely translates into what we think it does. It looks like a memorized faith rather than an internalized one. It hits and runs. It is all words and separation. I am not so sure it is the words that are needed now as much as the touchable, everyday expressions of the gospel that come through human hands, heart, and conversation. We need to be connecting with the world, not separating from it. We need to build bridges to our culture, not create fault lines.[3]
(*John Fischer*)

In a letter to the church in Corinth, Paul says that they (and by proxy, we) have been deemed ministers of reconciliation, which basically means we take the hand of our friend while taking Jesus' hand and connecting the two. Scripture alludes to the "priesthood of all believers," and the job description of a priest involves being a translator, an advocate, and a bridge builder—one who alleviates the chasm between "us" and "them" by helping people move toward Jesus.

SERVE

Worship, especially in America, has become a bit monochromatic in that it is equated with certain songs and a certain vernacular. I'm not slamming these forms of worship, but I think it is interesting that the word that most often shows up in Scripture for "attributing worth to God" is "avad" or "asab," which in the Hebrew, means "to serve." "Latreuo" is the Greek equivalent.

The more we experience and internalize His grace, the more we become an advocate and ambassador for His grace. Grace by proxy.

We have all been called to drop our proverbial nets and follow Jesus—to connect people to the Gospel Story, to sacrificially love and serve them with the cross in our peripheral vision, and to pay attention to what He is up to in the lives of those around us.

Proximity is everything. Again, Paul writes:

"Each one should use whatever gift he has received to serve others, faithfully administering God's grace in its various forms."
(1 Peter 4:10 NIV)

It's been said that the church exists to serve the world (with the assumption that the church exists first and foremost to serve Christ). It's not about us. It's not about our safety, our prosperity, our comfort, or how good we feel about ourselves. It's about going against the grain to serve the world around us. When we are aligned with the heart of Jesus, we will want nothing to do with entitlement, control, manipulation, arrogance, or power games. We exist to give ourselves away. Or, as John Piper says, "The greatness of Christian exiles is not success but service. We don't own culture, and we don't rule it. We serve it with brokenhearted joy and long-suffering mercy, for the good of man and the glory of Jesus Christ."

WATCH

"To watch" means to be intentional with friendships. It means listening to people, being awake to what God is doing—not just on the pages of Scripture or within the walls of the church, but in our classes, workplaces, neighborhoods, and random conversations. "To watch" means suppressing the urge to be selective with our vision, seeing only that with which we are comfortable.

When our eyes are open, we will see that everyone is hungry for what is true, what is real. "For I am about to do something new. See, I have already begun! Do you not see it?" (Isaiah 43:19 NLT). We will see that everyone is desperate to be loved and accepted, to feel that they belong. Everyone desires that elusive something (or someone) who will complete the picture, and who will give them a direction for their life.

Jesus essentially says, "Here I am. I'm standing at your door. Knocking. Loudly. I want to be found. The reason everything else leaves you feeling empty and dissatisfied is because I, and I alone, have come to bring you life." (See Revelation 3:20.)

The truth and grace of the Gospel is that Jesus not only saves people, but He transforms their lives through His ongoing presence in their lives. When our eyes are open to how God is working, moving, and protecting, it frees us up to take some chances, to do the unthinkable, to love instead of hate, to participate in what God wants to do in the lives of those around us.

Working with university students lends itself to some late nights. On one such occasion, I was anxious to get home after a long day but I felt like I needed to stop by a local coffee shop. On the one hand, this was not an unusual occurrence. I like coffee. I like coffee very much. Occasionally I feel the "need" to have a cup of this deliciously aromatic beverage.

But this "need" was different. This was not a caffeine-deprived prompting. I felt like God's Spirit wanted me to stop by the coffee house and, to be quite honest, I wasn't too happy about that and let Him know (in a nice way, of course). To be clear, I didn't hear an audible voice that sounded like James Earl Jones (which would have been very cool) telling me that I must stop, but I knew, you know? So in my head and heart, I had this conversation with God.

God: "You need to stop by the coffee shop."

Me: "With all due respect, I don't want to stop by the coffee shop. I want to go home and see my wife."

God: "Trust me on this. You need to stop by the coffee shop."

Me: "Okay, but I'm not happy about it."

So begrudgingly I parked the car and walked into the shop. The first thing I saw was a man sitting at a cafe table, facing the door, reading a book entitled, *Does God Exist?*

Me [to God]: "So . . . why am I here?" (No, I'm not really that clueless.)

Me [to café guy]: "Hey, that book looks interesting."

And then it was like the scene out of Acts 8 where Phillip comes alongside a chariot where an Ethiopian was reading a scroll and Phillip asks him, "Do you understand what you are reading?"

And the Ethiopian says, "How can I unless someone explains it to me?"

That wasn't word for word how our conversation went, but it was eerily similar. I asked about the book, which led to a conversation, which led to a few more conversations about God and life.

The Holy Spirit was up to something in that man's life and in an act of grace toward me, He gave me a literal front-row seat. Please don't hear that through the lens of self-centeredness. Sharing the reality of Christ in order to feel good about ourselves is spiritual narcissism. God doesn't need us to get His stuff done, and Scripture likes to point out that to accomplish His purposes, He uses the foolish things and the dregs of society and even a donkey, in Balaam's case.

God's Spirit prompts us to come alongside people so we can get a 3-D view of what God is up to, and that is why the process of legitimately loving someone enough to point him or her toward Jesus most always leads to spontaneous worship.

When you are driving home from the cafe, reliving the conversation, you realize that you had very little to do with the light bulb coming on, and you can barely contain the joy that is stirred up inside of you.

As God is pouring out His grace on our friend, it spills over on us, as well.

The more we experience and internalize His grace, the more we become an advocate and ambassador for His grace.

Grace by proxy.

We have all been called to drop our proverbial nets and follow Jesus—to connect people to the Gospel Story, to sacrificially love and serve them with the cross in our peripheral vision, and to pay attention to what He is up to in the lives of those around us.

Proximity is everything.

CONSIDER THIS

Grace by Proxy

1. What is Jesus inviting you into? What can you invite others into?

2. How can you live out the Great Commission "as you go?"

3. Have you seen the Gospel lived out in a way that created fault lines? Have you seen the Gospel lived out in a way that built bridges?

4. How has God shown you grace by allowing you a front-row seat in what He is up to in someone else's life?

1. Peterson, Eugene. *The Jesus Way*. Grand Rapids, MI: Eermans Publishing, 2007.
2. Zahariades, Jason. *The Off Ramp*. www.jzahariades.wordpress.com.
3. Fischer, John. *Fearless Faith: Living Beyond the Walls of Safe Christianity*. Eugene OR: Harvest House Publishing, 2002.

PROXIMITY IS
EVERYTHING.

Chapter Six

Stepping into the Grey

[Breaking through Stereotypes to Engage the Culture]

STEREOTYPES GO BOTH WAYS.

We were downtown one night at a coffee house and I noticed an elderly gentleman working on his laptop. I had seen him earlier eating some Italian food at La Scala's and being neighborly I asked him what he had had for dinner. He said he had the seafood special but had delayed dessert until he got to the coffee house where he could get some work done. I asked him what kind of work he did and he said he was a professor of Philosophy. Then he asked me what I did and I said I was a campus minister. He kind of grinned and said he was sorry and hoped I would recover from my shortcomings soon, and I laughed and patted his shoulder and made some comment about how I figured he would say something like that. Then I left and haven't been able to get the conversation out of my mind ever since.

Here's why.

That entire thirty seconds of conversation was based on stereotypes—the philosopher's stereotype of the Christian minister and the minister's stereotype of the philosopher. I wish I had a do-over. I wish there was a kind of conversation mulligan where I could do another take.

I wish I had asked him other questions like . . .

"What's your story? What makes you tick? Where did you grow up? Why did you decide to teach?"

"My knowledge of philosophy is somewhat limited. How would you describe your particular brand of thinking? From whom have you borrowed to form your unique brand of thought?"

"At the end of the day, does your rationale for living work for you in the sense of does it bring you transrational feelings like hope or joy?"

"What's your real view of spirituality in general, of Christianity specifically? Have you always felt that way or did something happen in your life that defined these feelings?"

"What are your assumptions about me? In what experiences or observations are those assumptions based?"

"Are you going to eat the rest of that Tiramisu because if not, well, can I have it?"

I wish I could ask those kinds of questions because he obviously had made assumptions about me based on a stereotype of ministers or Christians in general. But, in all honesty, I had made assumptions about him as well. There have been valuable words written the past few years that explain many of the nuances and layers of how people who are not yet followers of Jesus feel, in general, about those who are. The Christian snapshot often bleeds hatred, bigotry, and ignorance, and the disposition of Christians is often antithetical to what we see in Christ and what He taught His disciples.

When it comes to the world, there are a couple of different postures that Christians tend to gravitate toward, neither of which is actually in tune with God's heart. These two options represent a kind of binary response to grace, one legalistic and one abusive, and both perpetuate the negative stereotypes and perceptions of Christianity.

THE WAY WE ARE IN THE WORLD, OPTION 1:
US VS. THEM
(THE LEGALISTIC RESPONSE TO GRACE)

I was talking to a friend who said he is one of three Christians in his department and people can't stand the other two Christians because it is obvious that those two Christians can't stand non-Christians.

Sectarianism is the act of separating oneself from the world. When a virus was wreaking havoc on half of our family, our little boy announced, "Mom and I won't get sick because I put up a force field around us."

"Us vs. Them" is a self-imposed force field where a Christian sequesters himself from all the ugliness of the sinners around him and seeks to abstain from the culture he lives in.

He comes across as self-absorbed because he is more concerned with guarding his own righteousness than he is with the lives of those around him. He loves God but seems to have forgotten to love others. In seeking to build a fence of protection, he builds a fence of exclusion that seeks to sanitize rather than engage. His legalism disconnects him from the love of God as it is expressed for the brokenness of the world.

In an "Us vs. Them" world . . .

- It becomes easier for the Christian to shove opinions on people than actually listen to them.
- It becomes more about being right than loving the One who is Truth.
- It becomes easier to wear the mask of Christianity than bear the cross of Jesus.

An "Us vs. Them" worldview is predictable. It is safe. It is minimalistic. And it is ungodly.

THE WAY WE ARE IN THE WORLD, OPTION 2:

WE BECOME THEM
(THE INCOGNITO RESPONSE TO GRACE)

I asked a guy one time if it was hard to be a follower of Jesus in his particular major and he said, "Not at all. No one knows. I keep it to myself."

Syncretism is the subtle (or not so subtle) art of "fitting in" to the point where the Jesus follower is indistinguishable from the world they were once trying to reach. It is like a self-imposed witness relocation program where a person blends in so well that no one would ever suspect his true identity.

In conversation and interaction with non-Christians, faith is watered down to make it easier to swallow, or it is avoided altogether. The syncretist loves the world but has also bought into the world's view of life, which often is contrary to God's view. This person has usually either misinterpreted grace or has adopted a licentious view of it, and in seeking to express freedom, has ironically become blinded to the binding, destructive nature of that "freedom."

In a "We Become Them" worldview . . .

- It becomes easier to assimilate to the truth du jour, than to let God dictate truth on His terms.

- It becomes more about being accepted in order to fit in, than being distinctive in order to make a difference.

- It becomes easier to justify sin when discernment is suppressed in the name of accessibility.

It, too, is predictable, and safe, and minimalistic, and ungodly.

Too often the individual Christian and the corporate church chooses one of these two responses to culture—seclusion or morphing.

But there is a third way.

THE WAY WE ARE IN THE WORLD, OPTION 3:
WE ENGAGE WITH THEM
(THE APPROPRIATE RESPONSE TO GRACE)

"The kingdom of heaven is like yeast that a woman took and mixed into a large amount of flour until it worked all through the dough."
(Matthew 13:33 NIV)

Yeast. Basically, it is a fungus that quadruples the size of the flour dough by eating the sugar and as it ferments, it gives off carbon dioxide, which causes the dough to rise and smell like beer.

Throughout Scripture, yeast (or leaven) doesn't have a very good reputation. In Exodus, the Israelites were commanded to make bread without yeast during the Passover because it would be good for a quick getaway, but also because yeast was symbolic of anything that would contaminate God's people.

In another location, Jesus told His followers to be leery of the "yeast" of the Pharisees, in reference to their teaching that was focused on legalism instead of the truth of who God is. The same thing was going on in Galatia a few years later, so Paul writes:

"You were running a good race. Who cut in on you to keep you from obeying the truth? That kind of persuasion does not come from the one who calls you. A little yeast works through the whole batch of dough."
(Galatians 5:9 NIV)

So for the bulk of Scripture, leaven and yeast have been equated with contamination. And the metaphor is due to the fact that a little bit of yeast is like when somebody pees in the pool. The significance of the effect is larger than the amount of the substance itself.

But in Matthew 13, Jesus is standing in a boat teaching the people on the shore and He is describing to them what the Kingdom of Heaven is like using one metaphor after another. In the middle of these parables, Jesus says,

"God's Kingdom is like yeast that a woman works into the dough for dozens of loaves of barley bread—and waits while the dough rises."
(Matthew 13:33 MSG)

God's Kingdom is like yeast. That's curious.

Maybe Jesus is saying, "What if things were reversed?" Instead of just reactively avoiding the bad yeast that spreads like wildfire throughout culture like distortions of truth, false promises, and cheapened morals; what if the Kingdom of God was about proactively transforming culture to what God had intended for it to look like in the first place, proactively being yeast-like with His Truth and promises?

From the onset of creation, we read that everything was made with innate meaning, a reason for its existence. God called this culture "good," meaning "perfect" and dropped Adam and Eve into it. To be human is to be created in God's image as an inherently cultural being.

God's command was for people to care for and to keep creation going (Genesis 1:20-2:3). In other words, God's design was for humans to "do" culture; to create ways of life that reflect His love, grace, and truth. Our identity, the work we do, the meaning of our lives, the concerns we have for people and for the world—all of these things were included in this job description of being managers of culture.

So the Genesis story starts with a perfect culture. Sin screwed that up. With the crunch of the fruit in the Garden, culture was oriented away from God's intentions for it. Then came the whole Tower of Babel fiasco where people were feeling pretty good about their accomplishments and so God scattered them all over the place, thus fragmenting the population into various and autonomous language groups, belief structures, ethnicities, and practices.

Lately there is something else happening—a cross polli-nation or blending of cultural nuances that has produced a kind of cultural smoothie—a mixture of ideas, think tanks, the arts, ethnic backgrounds, and traditions.

In other words, culture, in one form or another, is inevitable. But how we view it and scrutinize it and attempt to transform it is all part of our participation in this revolution called the Kingdom of God.

The message we get from Romans is that . . .

Everything comes from Him.

Everything happens through Him.

Everything ends up in Him.

This is vital. God exists outside culture, invented culture, and personally entered the chaos of culture in order to redeem and restore culture for His Glory.

From day one, we humans have been commanded by God to participate in this forming and reforming culture. To do this effectively does not mean sequestering ourselves from cul-ture or creating our own safe bubble culture (i.e., sectarianism). Nor does it mean that we just morph into whatever the culture is dictating we should be or think or do (i.e., syncretism). In-stead we are called to engage culture:

"So here's what I want you to do, God helping you: Take your every-day, ordinary life—your sleeping, eating, going-to-work and walk-ing-around life—and place it before God as an offering. Embracing what God does for you is the best thing you can do for Him."

(Romans 12:1 MSG)

All in. Our whole existence; heart, soul, body, and mind must be committed to the Lord. The way we study, do business or research, the way we interact with our families, the way we spend our time, our conversations, our relationships, everything belongs to Him. Everything means everything. Paul is encour-aging us to learn to see things from the perspective of God's wholeness. The Hebrew word for this kind of completeness is "shalom" which is an all-encompassing, creative, covenantal kind of peace. We exist in the world and have been charged with a mission in that world of reconciling all things to God. Our ad-dress is here, in the world. It's our neighborhood, our dorm, our apartment complex, our classroom, our workplace. It's where our Christianity gets pushed out onto the stage and exposed for what it really is.

"Don't become so well-adjusted to your culture that you fit into it without even thinking. Instead, fix your attention on God. You'll be changed from the inside out. Readily recognize what He wants from you, and quickly respond to it. Unlike the culture around you, always dragging you down to its level of immaturity, God brings the best out of you, develops well-formed maturity in you."

(Romans 12:2 MSG)

Engagement means being observant. It means studying the culture and its influences, discerning what is congruent with God's Truth. It's like getting out Christmas lights to look for the bright bulbs mixed in with the burned out ones, calling a lie, "a lie," and calling a truth, "a truth." This includes an awareness that there are components of Christian subculture and politics and, if we're honest, of our own lives that are being pawned off as truth even when they aren't all that truthful. Subsequently, spiritual discernment opens the door for the discovery of beauty and truth in places where we didn't expect to find them.

Engagement means making friends, listening to people, being familiar with the arts, movies, music, world events, and causes—all with God on our minds and in our periphery. It means intentionally being in places where we have the opportunity and validity to redirect and reconcile humanity towards His Truth through His grace. All of this to say that evangelism becomes a lifestyle, not an act. More than ever, we need to actually be the Gospel instead of just standing up for it or talking about it.

Engagement involves understanding and emulating God's view of humanity and His heart for the world. It is recognizing the dichotomy that each person is both intricately created and desperately broken. Bono says it this way: "If I'm honest, I'm rebelling against my own indifference. I am rebelling against the idea that the world is the way the world is, and there's [nothing] I can do about it."

John Stott puts it this way:

> Jesus calls his disciples to exert a double influence on the society—a negative influence by arresting its decay and a positive influence by bringing light into its darkness. For it is one thing to stop the spread of evil; it is another to promote the spread of truth, beauty and goodness.[1]

All around us we see the effects of a world gone mad because it is disconnected from the God who made it and the Savior who Saved it. Can we do anything about the madness? Can we push against the effects of the Fall? Can we use our influence, money, studies, relationships, family ties, mobility, careers, brains, creativity, time, management and leadership skills, gifts, abilities, sensibilities, compassion, experiences, run-ins with grace, our messy past, and our eternal future . . . can we use it all to transform our part of the world for the glory and the cause of Christ?

Yes.

This is the third way. The way of engagement.

This is our calling, both individually and corporately.

In the broadest sense, engagement with the culture is about mobilizing the church toward the restorative work of God's Kingdom. The mission of the church is to bring (again, in John Stott's words) the "whole Gospel to the whole world." This is not a diversion from discipleship, but a furthering of both the Great Commission (Matthew 28:19-20 and Mark 16:15-16) to make disciples of all nations and God's cultural mandate (Genesis 1:26-28 and 2:15) to creatively participate in God's Kingdom via our work, relationships, art, and stewardship.

In the introduction, I stated that my desire was not to squeeze another "still-life" painting into the saturated gallery of evangelistic approaches and ideologies, but to offer some snapshots of this "Gospel in motion." Along the way, I've tried to construct a bit of a mosaic of what it means to individually come alongside neighbors, friends, and strangers in intentional ways.

But what about us collectively?

What does this "Gospel in motion" look like within the context of community?

What might it look like when the love we have for Jesus and one another spills out our doors and into the streets?

How do we engage culture as a church community?

Hans Kung suggests we do it this way:

A church which pitches its tents without constantly looking out for new horizons, which does not continually strike camp, is

93

being untrue to its calling. We must play down our longing for certainty, accept what is risky, and live by improvisation and experiment.[2]

"Accept what is risky and live by improvisation and experiment."

Sounds precarious.

Occasionally, I will propose these questions:

"Is there anything in my life that looks and feels like faith?"

"Is there anything about our church that looks and feels like faith?"

They are dangerous questions—a bit Abrahamic, really. I honestly don't ask them as often as I should because these particular questions tend to lead to unsettling, sometimes painful, changes to the script of my expectations. It is a venture away from entitlement and into the unknown and there aren't many guarantees (in the short term) about how it will go. Ultimately God gets the last word and restores everything, and the momentary pain gives way to eternal promises. But in the meantime, asking these questions will most likely lead us into new territory with exhaustion and disruption, mixed with the euphoria of stepping out in faith.

At one point, when my wife and I asked the question for ourselves, it led to adopting a child who had been severely neglected. He is an amazing, creative boy who unfortunately deals every day with the side effects of that neglect and though we love him with all we have, most days are really hard.

And that is the thing about faith—it's not a one-time deal that merely requires us to do something momentarily un-comfortable. Faith is ongoing. It is a lifelong process that brings us again and again to a point of decision, a narrowing of options, a place of trust.

Abraham trusted God and left everything he knew for the unknown, formidable, new terrain of a promise. The rest of the story, however, is that he had to keep trusting, he had to keep going. Some days he failed. Some days he doubted whether the risk was worth the difficulty. But ultimately he kept walking. His initial step of faith turned into tens of thousands of dusty, hope-filled steps.

"Is there anything in my life and about our church that looks and feels like faith?" It's an important question for us as individual Jesus followers, but it is just as critical for us to ask the question corporately. In fact, when several individuals within a church body are asking the question for themselves, inevitably the church will be affected.

Are we as a church community "accepting what is risky" or are we keeping to what is safe, what is programmatically proven?

Are we living by "improvisation and experiment" as we keep in step with the Holy Spirit and stay aligned with God's will and heart for this culture?

What would a corporate expression of "coming alongside" look like?

Are we willing to go there?

We are called to something different, something distinctive.

As one writer put it, we are called to be, "light bearers, grace mongers, and peddlers of hope."[3]

CONSIDER THIS
Stepping into the Grey

1. What assumptions do the people in your sphere of influence make about Christianity?

2. What assumptions do you make about those in your sphere of influence?

3. What does it mean in your life to effectively engage culture with truth and grace?

4. How do we relate to this world?

5. Do we really want to relate? Do we truly care about people?

6. "Is there anything in my life that looks and feels like faith?" What is your gut reaction to that question? How would you answer that question? Are you willing to pray to be in a place of reliance and trust?

7. "Is there anything about our church that looks and feels like faith?" How would your church community answer the question? What are some hindrances to a collective movement of faith in your church? Are you willing as a church to pray to be stretched beyond what is safe and predictable?

1. Stott, John. *The Message of The Sermon on The Mount*. Nottingham, England: Intervarsity Press, 1993
2. Kung, Hans. *The Church As the People of God*. London: Burns and Oates, 2001.
3. Bundschuh, Rick. *Don't Rock the Boat, Capsize It*. Colorado Springs, CO: Navpress, 2005.

AS ONE WRITER
PUT IT, WE ARE
CALLED TO BE,
"LIGHT BEARERS,
GRACE MONGERS,
AND PEDDLERS OF
HOPE."

Chapter Seven

Collective Engagement

[The Process of Coming Alongside
as a Community]

I want to share a bit of our church's story, definitely not as a template, but as an example of what it looks like to wrestle through the improvisational journey of faith together in an attempt to engage culture and love well.

I am not much of an artist or a musician or a writer, but I have always had a desire to infuse those things, along with hospitality, accessibility, (and yes) coffee into what we do as a ministry.

When I first came to campus, I used to hang out at a place called Blue Café. Although the shop officially closed at midnight, a few nights a week, the employees would choose to brew another pot of java and have discussions into the wee hours of the morning—those discussions centered around philosophy, religion, relationships, and life. There, in the Blue Café, coffee and conversation got in my blood—somewhat literally, I suppose.

A couple of years after coming on staff, I lobbied to turn the basement of one of our campus houses into a gathering space of sorts—neutral ground for people to hang out and talk, complete with round tables, live music, cool lights, coffee, and tea. Soon we began collecting artists to meet regularly. Sometimes we would write prose or poetry, other nights we would paint, take and develop photographs, or play music. Occasionally we would assemble a bunch of the work into a magazine or gallery exhibit. Bands were formed and started playing concerts all over campus and town. We even hosted a film festival.

As a group, we read and discussed the role of art in the church and the church's role and responsibility to express and extend God's beauty to the world. We saw how the arts could help the unchurched connect the dots to the Author of creativity and His love for this broken world. We felt that Jesus followers had a responsibility to express beauty with excellence and that the church should be a place that encouraged such activity. Then, one year, we decided the natural progression of all these components would be a street festival.

We had the first Starry Night Music and Arts Festival in a parking lot with a couple of bands and a few artists selling their wares. There were tables full of art supplies to encourage festival attendees to be creative and a few booths highlighting organizations that were trying to raise awareness about various social issues. Overhead hung several strands of Christmas lights and hand-painted banners which made the festival, well . . . festive.

The goal was to take the church out into the streets through the channels of art and music in order to build a context for relationships. We also wanted to serve the community by offering a different kind of experience than what they might be used to and by supporting local social causes, as well.

The festival went well. People were curious. Connections were made. We decided to do it again. And again.

Each year it grew a bit more—more bands, more merchants, more people, more conversation, and more impact. As the crowds grew, so did the work—more resources, more staff time, more organization, and more red tape. Each year we would give ourselves the permission to be done with the festival; then we would smile, take a deep breath, and go for it again. It felt like faith. It was a chance to break through stereotypes people had of church and provide a new context for engagement.

The atmosphere was electric. Literally. People who wanted nothing to do with church wanted to be there.

Every year I would hear the following words from various random people: "If only we could do this every week."

The words made me simultaneously laugh, shudder, and wonder: What about this environment draws people who would otherwise want nothing to do with Christians? What other context would allow us as a church to come alongside, serve, and affect culture in an intentional and relational way?

A coffee shop.

Throughout this whole process I had been looking for a space (other than a nasty basement) where we could reach outside of Campus House in order to make the collective "coming alongside" more accessible. Over a span of several years, I combed the city for the right kind of place. I talked to realtors, contacted potential donors, drew up designs, and dreamed about the possibilities—but it just never quite came together. The timing was off, the vision was incomplete, and a lot of pieces were missing. So as the result of some wise counsel, we shelved the idea.

A few years passed. Then one day, Jason Tennenhouse took the idea off the shelf.

A property on the edge of Purdue's campus became available, and we decided to pursue it. It was the perfect location—on a busy corner just off campus, a great old building in the middle of the bars and shops. We put our name in the hat and were informed that we were second in line. Typically my modus operandi on these kinds of things is to not get my hopes up so I won't be too devastated should it fall through. Still, there was a shot, and after dreaming of such things for so long, I was excited. About this time, our entire staff went on a mission trip to build a house together in Juarez, Mexico. While we were gone, the first people in line backed out. This would have been great news had there actually been cell phone reception in Juarez, Mexico. When the seller couldn't contact us, they sold the business to the third buyer on the list. It was disappointing to say the least, but we figured God had something else in mind.

Two and a half years later, we approached the owner and asked if he would be willing to sell the shop.

He said yes.

This put into motion a whirlwind of board meetings, negotiations, contracts, planning, designing, fund raising, menu making, and more.

We knew that it would be useless to pursue starting a restaurant venture without someone driving it who knew about such things. One of our alums had finished culinary school, and had just been offered a great job, but we called him and his wife anyway. Our proposal: "Would you be willing to come for a fraction of the pay and triple the work hours in order to take the risk of being a part of something new and exciting that feels a lot like faith?"

They said yes.

For months we prayed and put the puzzle pieces in place. On June 1, 2008, we signed the papers and picked up the keys. For the next forty-three days, some 250 volunteers would offer their time, skills, and service to a project which, at times, seemed as daunting as Nehemiah's reconstruction of the walls of Jerusalem (which took fifty-two days, by the way, and luckily we had no "dung gate" to repair). Students, parents, friends from other churches and campus ministries, amateurs and professionals, sometimes total strangers dismantled "what had been" and began framing "what would be." A few months earlier we had narrowed a list of three hundred possible names to "Greyhouse Coffee and Supply Company."

In Mark 12:30, Jesus boils the Ten Commandments down to two. Love God. Love your neighbor. The second flows from the first. Hospitality is a working out of the Gospel. This shop would give us a daily space to practice it as a community outside the church walls, on turf that is unpredictable and raw with people who are hungry for what only Jesus can give. We wanted to practice what it might look like for the church to step into the grey with light, grace, and hope.

What is true about each person who comes through the Greyhouse doors is that they are created in the image of God, and with that DNA comes a longing that ultimately only He can satisfy.

Early in the storyline of Genesis, we see clearly that sin separates people. People are lonely and isolated, desiring to be known, to be a part of something. Henri Nouwen has written that one of the gifts we bring to the world as Christians is "making our lives available to others." Hospitality reverses the effects of the fall, creating a bridge back to the truth and grace of the Father.

As Christine Pohl writes:

> Early Christian writers claimed that transcending ethnic and social differences by sharing meals, homes, and worship with persons of different backgrounds was a proof of the truth of the Christian faith. For most of the history of the Christian church, hospitality meant a recognition of a person's worth and common humanity.[1]

When people find that there is room for them, that they are welcomed and valued and known, when we share our lives and go beyond what is expected, then there is a good possibility that they will get a taste of what the unconditional love of Christ must be like.

Years ago, I read these words from Rick Richardson, which increasingly characterized what we were experiencing:

> Experience comes before explanation. Belonging comes before believing.[2]

What we felt God was creating among us was a place for people to belong and a place for us to "practice hospitality" (Romans 12:13). It was a place to share a cup of cold water or a cup of hot Ethiopian Yirgacheffe in His name (Matthew 10:42).

THIRD WAY

The phrase "the third way" has been used (okay, overused) to describe everything from political movements to dog training, but it is does accurately describe something that doesn't quite fit. Generally it is the harder way. The poles are easier, more defined. In our case, we knew that we didn't want to do a "Christian" coffee shop. On the other hand, we didn't want to just do a coffee shop.

One patron put it this way. "If you were attempting to go under the radar and just have a business, then you would have great coffee and crepes, but for what? If you were attempting to do a typical 'Christian coffee shop,' then nine tenths of these people wouldn't be in here; but the fact that most everyone knows who owns this place and yet they want to be here—now you have validity to speak into their lives."

The third way takes intentionality. It takes ownership. It takes work. It takes excellence. It takes love.

Romans 12 encapsulates the vision: "Love from the center of who you are; don't fake it. Be good friends who love deeply; practice playing second fiddle. Don't burn out; keep yourselves fueled and aflame. Be alert servants of the Master, cheerfully expectant. Don't quit in hard times; pray all the harder. Help the needy; be inventive in hospitality" (Romans 12:9–13 MSG).

If our primary way to share Christ is through relationships, then we felt we couldn't limit the radius of those relationships to those who come to our church building. It is about going to the culture, not demanding they come to us.

As a church, we had been pursuing what Christ meant when He talked about the upside-down Kingdom of God where the first are last and the last are first, where grace becomes a way of life, where community is authentic. This was a chance to try to live that out, to put "some skin in the game." We had dreamed specifically of a community space where Kingdom theology gets lived out.

- A place that is accessible to people who may never walk through the doors of a church.
- A place that serves a really good cup of coffee, but also excels as a business, building relationships and trust with vendors, the city, and surrounding businesses.
- A place to put life on "pause" for a few minutes.
- A place where people celebrate passing the final and getting engaged, but also a place where people drift when life is falling apart.
- A place to engage in conversation that goes beyond the surface.
- A place where people feel a part of a community; neutral ground where people come to know the love of Jesus by being around His followers.
- A place where employees actually care about what they do and have a genuine love for customers.
- A place where people feel at home as soon as they walk in; where people feel known.
- A place where the love of Jesus is demonstrated through the skill of listening and the art of asking good questions.
- A place that connects people to Him through being connected to people they can respect and trust.
- A place that is accepting of people with different opinions and protects people's dignity.
- A place of strong conscience (social and environmental) that exists to serve the community and world.

- A place that inspires people to create and do good and think bigger than themselves.

- A place that uses the arts as a language to communicate truth in a way that can be embraced by the unchurched.

The response to Greyhouse from the Purdue and Greater Lafayette communities has been incredibly affirming. There has been an average of over five hundred customers a day, not only ordering coffee, crepes and gelato, but also experiencing something distinctive in the way they are served, known, and valued.

For the Greyhouse staff, it's not just a place to work. It is a chance to be a part of what God is up to in the lives of each person who walks in. They are intentional about hospitality and have garnered the reputation for serving in a way that goes the extra mile. They get to know the customers and their stories. They help people feel connected and loved. All of this creates a unique environment that allows customers to feel at home. One student from Egypt always sits at the counter next to the staff just because he loves to eavesdrop on their conversations.

A Greyhouse regular wrote this on his blog: "A customer goes to a coffee shop to find a relaxed environment to do light work, read a book, or meet with friends—all of which has a common denominator of relaxation. This is not accomplished by complex business formulas and techniques, but in very small but noticeable everyday acts. For example, employees at Greyhouse seem to actually enjoy working there, which is essential to offering good customer service. At night right before closing, they don't ask the customers to leave in five minutes. They ask whether they can get them anything else before they close."

But there is ministry internally as well. The staff meet regularly to connect with each other and to remind one another of the big picture—why Greyhouse exists. They study the Word together and pray for one another. There is an openness with one other, a caring that is woven throughout the nature of the place. They each feel ownership in the mission of Greyhouse. They love God in a way that spills out into how they treat each other. And they love one another in a way that demonstrates God living in them.

"If we love one another, God lives in us and his love is made complete in us."

(1 John 4:12 NIV)

The environment has led to customers feeling an ownership in Greyhouse as well: people offering open seats to total strangers, sharing their insights on the community board, explaining to their friends the nuances of the shop or retelling what they have learned of the disparity that exists in the global coffee business. Greyhouse is designed for conversation and at any given time, there is most likely a cacophony of discussion about politics, electrical engineering, and a passage of Scripture. It's not unusual to overhear a conversation about a weekend party next to two people praying together. We're not asking people to clean up their act. It's not about just serving coffee to nice people. It is about coming alongside people and each day extending grace in a thousand ways in a space that invites curiosity.

When the church is willing to collectively step out in faith with the purpose of pointing people toward Jesus, they find themselves connected to and participating in what God is already up to outside the church walls.

The Greyhouse experiment has opened the door for other possibilities of faith-driven improvisation as well. For the last few years, we have felt that a significant niche of our ministry is helping students think about their lives (vocations, gifts, passions, abilities, skills, resources) in light of God's Kingdom.

It's something that is very much a part of the vernacular of our large group teaching, small group discussions, and one-on-one conversations.

We started an annual (hands-on) conference called Engaging Culture where university students and twenty-somethings gather in Indianapolis to connect with specific issues and think about the possibilities for meeting those needs. Each November we have "Mobilization Week" where we give students time to think and pray through their own stories, identity, and calling in light of Scripture, and have brainstorming sessions complete with an enormous dry erase board. On the board, students list needs that exists globally and locally as well as various resources, skills, and ideas people have for meeting those needs. Some of these ideas have turned into initiatives and some of these initiatives have come to fruition.

For instance, the need of a local family for a handicap-accessible van led students to organize an outdoor concert and awareness campaign that raised the needed funds.

Students who wanted to develop a system for using their leftover meal swipes to feed the hungry, both locally and globally, led to them forming a campus-wide program called "Swipe Out Starvation" which, to date, has raised thousands of dollars for local and international hunger needs.

A couple of years ago, our ministry decided to formalize this process of empowering college students to put their faith into action. We rented space upstairs from Greyhouse and part of our staff who are gifted in ideation and graphic design moved in to form GreyMob.

GreyMob is part design studio, part think tank, and part idea accelerator—kind of a ministry Research & Development department. The idea is to come alongside passionate students who have big ideas and give them the resources and guidance to start new, faith-inspired, and socially conscious initiatives. God seems to be building up a generation desperate to use their education and gifts to make a real and sustained impact on culture, through their experience of being personally transformed by the Gospel. The church has an opportunity to encourage, pray for, and facilitate that impact.

So back to the Hans Kung quote: "A church which pitches its tents without constantly looking out for new horizons, which does not continually strike camp, is being untrue to its calling. We must play down our longing for certainty, accept what is risky, and live by improvisation and experiment."[3]

As individual collectives, as the church of (insert appropriate city or town or corn field), where are we pitching our tent? Are we corporately sequestering ourselves from society for reasons of safety, comfort, or control? Are we corporately assimilating ourselves into society in such a watered-down way that there is nothing distinctive about us?

Or are we practicing the third way, the harder way, the way of engagement?

"Even though I am free of the demands and expectations of everyone, I have voluntarily become a servant to any and all in order to reach a wide range of people: religious, nonreligious, meticulous moralists, loose-living immoralists, the defeated, the demoralized—whoever. I didn't take on their way of life. I kept my bearings in Christ—but I entered their world and tried to experience things from their point of view. I've become just about every sort of servant there is in my attempts to lead those I meet into a God-saved life. I did all this because of the Message. I didn't just want to talk about it; I wanted to be in on it!"

(1 Corinthians 9:10–13 MSG)

We want to be in on it. We want to lead people into a God-saved life.

In this chapter, I have tried to describe a bit of what the process has looked like in our setting—wrestling, praying, dreaming, and moving to reach out to this distinct part of culture at this time with this intrinsic set of passions, skills, desires, and messiness. I believe God is calling the church to work within each particular context (campus, city, culture) and among our particular people to affect the spiritual, physical, emotional, material, and social needs that we can reach.

- To pay attention to what is going on around us.
- To be disrupted and leveled by the Holy Spirit.
- To have compassion and urgency for those who have yet to experience the love of Jesus.
- To be motivated to respond in a way that is in step with the Spirit.

Whatever this looks like in each particular setting, whether an after-school literacy program, delivering meals to people with HIV, or a wine bar that is intentional about relational ministry—can we collectively pray and dream and move? Faith is not the enemy of discernment and though there are a thousand pitfalls to look out for along the way and definitely no warranties, are we willing to try? Are we willing to fail? Are we willing to risk?

When the love of God fills our hearts, we act out of what the Spirit is doing in us and through us. We live out the Gospel together and take it to neutral ground.

It is the way of Jesus in the grey.

CONSIDER THIS
Collective Engagement

1. What does it look like in your setting to "come along-side" corporately?

2. What are the particular needs that exist in your community? Can you identify a possible niche that you as a church community (or even a few of you within your church community) might fill in order to address those needs?

3. How might you leverage your particular collection of gifts, passions, abilities, skills, and resources?

4. What about globally? Is there a certain region or people group, or a specific need that exists in that part of the world to which your church community can creatively bring the wholeness of the Gospel?

1. Pohl, Christine. *Making Room: Recovering Hospitality as a Christian Tradition*. Grand Rapids, MI: WIlliam B. Eerdmans, 1999.
2. Richardson, Rick. *Evengelism Outside The Box*. Downers Grove, IL: Intervarsity Press, 2000.
3. Kung, Hans. *The Church*. Colorado Springs, CO: Image Books, 1976.

WE LIVE OUT THE
GOSPEL TOGETHER
AND TAKE IT TO
NEUTRAL GROUND.
IT IS THE WAY OF
JESUS IN THE GREY.

Chapter Eight

Outside-in

[Making Room for Those in the Grey]

The term "no man's land" was first used in the early four-teenth century in medieval England. It was the name given to a dump outside the north walls of London where criminals were executed and their bodies left on display as a warning to others. The land could never be claimed for ownership and therefore became known as "no man's land."

Project the same idea from this bit of gruesome medie-val history onto a page from Israel's history. The law that God handed down to Moses had references to a sort of "no man's land" as well, except God used the phrase, "outside the camp." It was a space that served as the community landfill, the temple incinerator, and communal toilet; but it also served as a place of execution for blasphemers and a place of residence for certain people within the Israelite community. It was a kind of buffer zone for those who had become ceremonially unclean and had to be separated from the community because of disease or sin. It was home to those from pagan tribes who had helped Israel in some way, but were still considered unclean and "outsiders."

Here are a few examples from the Old Testament:

"All of you who have killed anyone or touched anyone who was killed must stay outside the camp seven days."
(Numbers 31:19 NIV)

"Designate a place outside the camp where you can go to relieve yourself."
(Deuteronomy 23:12 NIV)

"So the young men who had done the spying went in and brought out Rahab, her father and mother and brothers and all who belonged to her. They brought out her entire family and put them in a place outside the camp of Israel."
(Joshua 6:23 NIV)

For some, life in this "no man's land" was only for a few days and then they could be considered "clean" again and welcomed back into the community, but for others, life in the landfill was a permanent home. Because of their ethnicity, disease, or crime, they were forever separated from the community. This meant being disconnected from relationships, from the ability to do business, and from community life in general, which included being cut off from corporate worship, feasts, prayers, and sacrifices. Life "outside the camp" wasn't just geographical—it was an isolation that was all-encompassing. It was a place of death in every sense of the word.

In the New Testament, the writer of Hebrews is addressing Christians who, until recently, had been Jews. The whole book is brilliant in the way the writer weaves the storyline of Israel together with how Jesus completes the tapestry of the law and feasts, the sacrificial system, the tabernacle and temple, the words of the prophets, and the Kingdom and promises of God. The Jewish Christians reading the book had been raised to consider everything "outside the camp" as unclean and evil. It was the part of town one avoided at all costs. To be there, around those people and that filth would mean putting one's own religious status in jeopardy. Again, anything or anyone who was considered unclean or an "outsider" had to be kept away from the "insiders"—had to be kept outside the camp.

With that knowledge, these words would have hit like a ton of bricks:

"The high priest carries the blood of animals into the Most Holy Place as a sin offering, but the bodies are burned outside the camp. And so Jesus also suffered outside the city gate to make the people holy through His own blood. Let us, then, go to Him outside the camp, bearing the disgrace He bore."

(Hebrews 13:11–13 NIV)

"Outside-in" was a central theme Jesus carried throughout His ministry. He told stories about a loving shepherd who went after a single lost sheep, a tenacious woman who turned her house upside down to find a lost coin, a grieving father who waited day after day beside the road for his rebellious son to come home—not so he could then unload his frustrations, curses, and judgment, but rather lavish his forgiveness and grace in the form of a party.

Jesus told a story about a great banquet where the usual attenders, the entitled, party-fatigued "insiders" made up all kinds of excuses to get out of the obligatory attendance. As a result, the doors were opened wide to those who typically would never get an invitation—the lame, the lost, the disenfranchised, the "outsiders."

At the outset of His ministry, Jesus' opening words, "Repent, for the Kingdom of God is at hand" (Matthew 3:2 ESV), was the prologue to a new storyline. "Insider" status would no longer be based on one's family tree, title, or earned credit, but would now come through an invitation to a crucifixion tree, receiving grace and a new name. Being undone by the Truth and repenting of any and all distortions of that Truth manifested in sin, the former "outsider" would now have a placard at the table.

Jesus spent His ministry coming alongside the outcasts, the broken, the skeptics, the poor, the rednecks, and the unclean, with the excellent news that, through Him, their status as "outsiders" could change—they could be known, loved, valued, and included. Jesus spent a majority of His time "outside the camp" and the time He spent with those "inside the camp" was mostly spent realigning their view as to who was an "insider." The culmination of this paradigm was Golgotha; the dump outside of Jerusalem where the animal carcasses were burned, where people dumped their sewage, where the unclean and most marginalized of the "outsiders" lived, where Jesus was crucified.

"Let us, then, go to Him outside the camp, bearing the disgrace He bore," says the writer.

Those words were written for a Jewish audience, but the principle applies to the rest of us as well. We must go to where Jesus is. If we are going to follow Him, we can't be selective about the destination. "Let us go to Him, outside the camp"— outside the bubble of religious structure, outside what is safe or comfortable, outside the usual guest list. We must go to where Jesus is. Yes, theologically, He is everywhere, but don't we tend to be selective with which parts of "everywhere" we wish to join Him?

As removed as we are from the context of the words in Hebrews, they are just as poignant for us. The lines of "outside" and "inside" are just as bold, even if the reasons are different. There are those who have chosen to be "outsiders" because they see themselves as intellectually or culturally superior to Christians or because they have had a bad experience with "insiders." Perhaps they've experienced some sort of betrayal or apathy or hypocrisy from the church or a believer, and perhaps this experience has left them with a bad taste in their proverbial mouths. Their whole stereotype of "insiders" may quite possibly be: "If that's an 'insider,' then I don't really care to be an 'insider.'"

There are also people who are "outsiders" because they believe they're not good enough to be an "insider"—to receive forgiveness, to be in community. The depth of their brokenness or past or sin keeps them outside the walls, removed from the hope that God (and His followers) could ever possibly accept them, welcome them, and love them.

Both sentiments are heartbreaking considering the whole reason that Jesus took on the flesh and blood and limitations of humanity, the whole meaning of a blood-stained cross and empty grave, is to let "outsiders" know the really good news that they don't have to be "outsiders" anymore.

Both of the camps outside the walls need a new perspective. The ones who think they're too good to be "insiders" need to come to terms with the truth that they (indeed, like the believers who screwed up), need a Savior; that they are not worthy of salvation, but instead have earned death.

"For all have sinned and fallen short of the glory of God."
(Romans 3:23a ESV)

"The wages of sin is death."
(Romans 6:23 ESV)

And then, like the ones who already "know" they're not good enough, they need to be pleasantly surprised by the subsequent reality of God's grace and love and His redemptive work on the cross.

"But the free gift of God is eternal life in Christ Jesus our Lord."
(Romans 3:23b ESV)

Jesus said, "I am the door. If anyone enters by me, he will be saved. . . . " (John 10:9 ESV). Jesus is the one and only door, the way from the outside to the inside, from death to life, from despair to hope, from isolation to community, from lost to found.

You know this, don't you? It's pretty likely that if you are reading this particular book, you've experienced and/or are presently experiencing this movement from "outsider" to "insider." But once people move from "outsider" to "insider," that is not the end of the story. "Insider" doesn't mean you are part of an exclusive club, it means you are part of a movement, a revolution, a mission. "Coming alongside" means that those who are now "insiders" through the grace of Jesus must (in Louie Giglio's words) "keep the door open" for the "outsiders," for those who have yet to taste, experience, and receive that grace.[1]

Paul expounds on this idea in his letter to the church in Colossae.

"Be wise in the way you act toward outsiders; make the most of every opportunity. Let your conversation be always full of grace, seasoned with salt, so that you may know how to answer everyone."
(Colossians 4:5–6 NIV)

Be wise in the way you act toward outsiders.

And make the most of every opportunity.

I got a phone call from a guy who wanted some ideas about how his church, of people mostly over the age of sixty, might reach out to university students. I asked him about the church's situation and he replied that the church building was close to campus, that parking on campus was hard to come by, and in between the church building and campus were several hundred apartments housing students. I asked him about the church's resources and he replied that they owned a bus and thought "perhaps they could use the bus to transport students to campus."

I thought that was an excellent idea.

Unfortunately, he continued.

"So I thought we could get students to park in our parking lot and then, if they agree to come to a weekly Bible study, they can ride to class for free."

"If/then" statements can be somewhat limiting.

"What if" questions, on the other hand, are pretty exciting.

In this particular scenario, what if there weren't a prerequisite of Bible study attendance in order to ride the bus?

What if students were simply welcome to use the parking lot and jump on the bus each day? What if Roy the bus driver (Roy just sounds like a bus driver's name to me) determined to learn the names of his riders and some of their stories as well? What if the church lobby became the "bus station" and the retired folks took turns making muffins and hanging out with the college students as they waited for Roy to return for his next load?

What if, over the course of the year, this intentionality included celebrating birthdays or inviting stranded students to Thanksgiving meals. What if these folks picked up on the cues when a student was having a rough day and offered to listen and to pray? What if, on occasion, a student was curious about what motivated the muffins and free rides and the obvious joy and hope with which these old people lived life? What if, on such occasion, these folks simply told them about the love of Jesus? What if some of these (now intrigued) students started asking if they could possibly have some sort of group to read the Bible and find out more about this Jesus?

What are the "what ifs?" for you?

How can you keep the door open for those around you?

How might this change the way you and I pray?

Again, Paul writes to the Colossians:

"Devote yourselves to prayer, being watchful and thankful. And pray for us, too, that God may open a door for our message, so that we may proclaim the mystery of Christ, for which I am in chains. Pray that I may proclaim it clearly, as I should."
(Colossians 4:2-4 NIV)

Devote yourselves to prayer.

Pray for an open door.

The word "devote" doesn't leave much room for a minimalistic, occasional, "whenever I get around to it," kind of prayer. We are to pray with our eyes proverbially open, being watchful and thankful. When we are watchful, we are aware of and can pray specifically about the circumstances in a person's life and the potential obstacles they might have to the Gospel. We can be truly thankful for the people for whom we are praying. We can pray with a vision of how God, in His graciousness and creativity, might use the circumstances in their lives to lead them toward an openness and curiosity about Him.

Paul pleaded for the church to pray for an open door to the Gospel and that, whenever he spoke about Jesus, he would do so with clarity. He did not want to get in the way of people coming to know and love Christ.

We, too, can pray for opportunities to serve and love people and for chances to talk freely about the impact that God has made in our lives. There is a time to speak, to use words to proclaim the hope of life in Jesus and we can pray for discernment to speak the right word at the right time to the right person; not manipulating the conversation in order to give a rehearsed sales pitch, but listening as to why they might be on the "outside looking in" when it comes to the way of Jesus and then speaking into that. We can pray for wisdom about when to share our own story of God's grace and patience in the midst of our questions, doubts, and struggles.

To come alongside "outsiders" will mean that we enter the grey, "no man's land," with the good news of inclusion through the One self-described as not only the Way, Truth, and Life, but also the Door—Jesus the Door, welcoming "outsiders" to come in where there is light, freedom, and room. The Hebrew word for salvation is "yasha" and means "to create room, to make space, as if by knocking down walls."

A few years ago, I had the opportunity to take a group of students to New Zealand to do various forms of ministry in the city of Auckland. I recruited some of our musicians to go along and we had the opportunity to play our music in church basements and coffee houses, including one in the middle of the red-light district (which is another story for another time). The place we had hoped to play was Temple Bar. In the middle of Auckland on Queen Street, this venue had live bands every night of the week and was considered the place to play in the city.

Assuming that the chances were slim to none, we wandered in one day, explained to the manager that we were in the country for three weeks and would love the chance to play a show.

The manager shot us a wary glance and said, "You know we are booked, three bands a night for the next three months, right?"

"Yea, we figured it was a long shot. Thanks anyway."

As we turned to leave, he shocked us with the words: "Hold on a minute there. We'll fit you in. We'll make room for you."

So at 6:30 p.m. on a Wednesday night, we played Temple Bar.

"We'll make room for you."

These are words that are sweet to the taste. They are words of inclusion, grace, and hospitable love.

These words are the essence of the Gospel, where the door is opened and the "outsiders" are invited inside.

CONSIDER THIS
Outside-in

1. Who are the "outsiders" in your community (socially, economically, physically, spiritually, ethnically)?

2. Who are the "outsiders" in your life (work place, neighborhood, classroom)?

3. What is keeping them "outsiders?"

4. Is there room in your life for others?

5. How can you make room for others in your life?

6. Who specifically will you make room for this week?

1. Giglio, Louie. "Our House: Doorholders Unite." May 14, 2012. Recording.

THESE ARE WORDS
THAT ARE SWEET
TO THE TASTE.
THEY ARE WORDS
OF INCLUSION,
GRACE, AND
HOSPITABLE LOVE.

Chapter Nine

Already in Progress

[Participating in What God Is Up To in the Lives of Those around You]

I THOUGHT I MIGHT POSSIBLY DIE.

Iwas working late in my office one night. The rest of the staff had gone home for the evening but had left the building unlocked. Around 10:00 p.m. a college student I had never seen before burst into my office and slammed the door. He was huge and had a wincing kind of expression on his face that was hard to read—he was either about to cry or rip my head off. (And did I mention that I was the only one in the building?) I suppose most people who find themselves in a similar situation would lean toward "fight" or "flight," but neither seemed to be an option as the guy was at least twice my weight and blocking my only exit. In what was probably more self-preservation than actual interest, I squeaked out some words in a voice that, under duress, probably sounded a bit pre-pubescent: "Can I help you?"

He pulled up a chair, sat his hulking body in it, and said, "I want to become a Christian."

"Excuse me?" (It's not exactly what I was expecting to hear.)

"I want to become a Christian. My life is screwed up, and I need God in a desperate way. I want to be baptized—tonight."

"Tonight? Are you sure, because if you could wait till Sunday then we coul—"

"Tonight."

I surmised that he was rather anxious to be baptized.

As a bit of background, in the book of Acts, conversion was nearly always accompanied by water baptism, and the practice of our ministry is to baptize by immersion. This usually takes place at a local church or in a borrowed horse trough or a pool surrounded by the church community. There are prayers, testimonies, and cake. It's a big deal—a mix of worship and the best kind of party. But this was 10 o'clock on a Tuesday night, and it was just the Hulk and me.

I called a local pastor and asked to borrow his church baptistry, and he was kind enough to give permission and agree to open the door for us. However, the Hulk and I drove across town and made our way through the darkened church building (I couldn't find the lights) to the baptistry only to find that it was completely dry.

I turned to him. "So now what do you want to do?"

"I'm not waiting. We're going to the Wabash."

"Excuse me? (Again, it was not exactly what I was expecting and definitely not what I wanted to hear.)

More background. This was the first of March in Indiana and the Wabash River was somewhere between eight and twelve feet above flood stage which meant a couple of things, neither of which excited me all that much: the water would be incredibly cold, and the current would be dangerously swift. However, even if it had been 2:00 p.m. on a cloudless day in July, the Wabash River is not a place one would generally want to bathe. It's not exactly what you would call a pristine water source. It's rumored to be full of all kinds of pollutants and run-offs that mutate fish into one-eyed, three-legged creatures, and it is known to leave a membrane-like residue and stench on one's skin that is reminiscent of raw sewage. I honestly believe that, had the Ethiopian eunuch wheeled his chariot to the Wabash River and said, "There's water, what prevents me from being baptized?" Phillip would have cringed and suggested an alternative. That is just my opinion.

Regardless of my hesitancy, there would be no deterring this guy. We drove to the boat ramp and parked the car in a location where the headlights would be able to illuminate the fog (yes, there was also fog) enough to perhaps find a lull in the current. I talked to him about what it means to become a follower of Jesus. He repented of his sin, confessed that Jesus is God's Son, and prayed for Jesus to save him from the destructive chaos and to become the priority of his life. Then we made our way into the water.

In a matter of only a couple of steps, the river was up to his waist and, subsequently, up to my shoulders. The temperature of the water was so cold that it took my breath away, but I somehow managed to say, "Name . . . Father . . . Son . . . Spirit . . . baptize . . . " and dunked his head under. That is when the current caught him, and by "him," I mean both of us. I grabbed him around the neck and held on for the ride thinking (for the second time that evening) that I would soon see Jesus face to face. It would be a rather unique way to go, really, and for the guy I was baptizing, incredibly efficient: from the watery grave to new life, from the polluted Wabash to the crystal-clear river of life flowing from the throne of God. Metaphors were swirling in my head as fast as the current that pulled us; and then a few seconds later, our feet touched down on a sand bar and we came out of the river choking and sputtering water, laughing and yelling literal praises to God.

Our baptism services have all seemed rather tame since then.

I tell you that story to both illustrate and reinforce the idea (in the first chapter) that, in the process of coming alongside people, we are joining something "already in progress." If you stumble upon a movie "already in progress" or a conversation "already in progress," it would behoove you to listen for a bit, to pay attention to what has already happened, to collect pieces of the storyline, and then to get caught up. Not the other way around.

The same is true in the art of intentionally coming alongside others. We pay attention in order to build upon what God has been doing in that person, directly through His Spirit and indirectly through other Jesus followers, experiences, and circumstances. There is something very organic about that. Paul alludes to it in one of his letters.

In Paul's first letter to the church in Corinth, he is addressing the dysfunction of the church and their focus on Christian rock stars instead of Jesus. Some were claiming to be followers of Paul, some Apollos, others had Simon Peter T-shirts and bobble-heads.

Paul writes:

"Now you're just being ridiculous. Who are we?" "We are only God's servants through whom you believed the Good News."
(1 Corinthians 3:5 NLT)

He then describes the "coming alongside" process and the roles that people and God play in that process.

"Each of us did the work the Lord gave us. I planted the seed in your hearts, and Apollos watered it, but it was God who made it grow. It's not important who does the planting, or who does the watering. What's important is that God makes the seed grow. The one who plants and the one who waters work together with the same purpose."
(1 Corinthians 3:5–8 NLT)

Sometimes we plant, sometimes we water, but God brings the growth. He is the One who saves. This truth should bring both a sense of urgency and a sense of freedom to evangelism.

Yes, urgency.

A sense of urgency is really another way to define our motivation for evangelism. It is both a response to the grace we've been given (the Good News that we can't keep quiet) and authentic mercy for people, which God produces in us when we are keeping in step with the Holy Spirit. We feel deeply. We are moved to action. We "can't not" bring the whole Gospel to the whole person, to the whole world. We have an urgency that is both immediate and eternal. We are empathetic and try (individually and/or corporately) to meet the physical, emotional, and material needs of people as we hold out the soul-saving, eternal truth of Christ and the reality of a grace-stained cross. We care about their present pain as well as what happens to them after they die.

The reality of hell, in my opinion, is not a great evangelistic tool for trying to scare someone into conversion. I do not think the use of fear is a very sustainable motivation in that it doesn't necessarily lead to true discipleship and is disconnected from the love of God, which both casts out fear (1 John 4:8) and compels us (2 Corinthians 5:14). However, the reality of hell can be an effective and gut-wrenching impetus for the believer who must break through the obstacles of his own apathy or fear of rejection in order to get this "light" to people who are saturated in darkness.

There is definitely a time to speak, to warn, to intervene, to go to whatever extremes to get the attention of someone we love who is headed toward destruction. When this is authentic, it comes from a place of deep compassion rather than judgment, and is validated by a persistent presence and an ongoing willingness to keep "showing up," which both accompanies and gives gravity to our insistent words.

There is a sense of urgency.

Simultaneously, there is a sense of freedom.

"What's important is that God makes the seed grow."
(1 Corinthians 3:6 NLT)

If it isn't up to us to save people, to seal the deal, to get the lost to say the prayer or get baptized—if that really is God's role and not ours—then we are freed up to come alongside them with discernment and with a posture of humility. We are free to adjust our speaking, praying, and serving in a way that is sensitive, not only to the Holy Spirit, but to the person we are trying to reach.

We are freed up to be honest with our lives. When life is incredibly difficult or we are in a season of wrestling with God, we don't have to give the illusion that we have everything figured out or put together in order to "be a good witness." That distortion is actually a horrible witness because it is dishonest and paints a picture of religion-soaked, outward appearances rather than authentic discipleship. When we are free to be real, behavior management and compartmentalization give way to validity and accessibility. There is a sense of freedom; a freedom to love well, listen well, speak well, and build well.

In verse 9, Paul switches metaphors from the garden to the construction site.

> **"Because of God's grace to me, I have laid the foundation like an expert builder. Now others are building on it. But whoever is building on this foundation must be very careful. For no one can lay any foundation other than the one we already have—Jesus Christ."** *(1 Corinthians 3:10–11 NLT)*

He goes on to say that people will build on the foundation of Jesus with a "variety of materials" and those materials will have different strengths and textures and functions. So, in the church's work of building upon the true foundation of Christ in people's lives, there are different people with different roles, working with different tools and at different times to bring together (with the strength and power of the Holy Spirit) this spiritual building, this life that is saved by, restored by, and devoted to Christ.

For a few years in a row, I took different teams of college students to Worcester, England, to work with some friends who were planting a church. Like most cities in Europe, Worcester has a beautiful, majestic church building in its town center and each trip we would spend a morning at the Worcester Cathedral exploring the crypt, examining the stained glass, journaling, and praying. It was amazing to think about the details, design, and craftsmanship that went into the construction at a time when tools and methodology were so limited. Our host told us it took over four hundred years to build. Can you imagine working your whole life on a project whose end result neither you nor your fourteen generations of grandkids would ever see? It took hundreds of individuals over a span of centuries, each doing their little part with a vision of a beautifully constructed place of worship.

In a similar way, we come alongside people with the vision of what their lives can become when they are radically altered by the Gospel. Once in awhile, we get to see the fruit of their repentance and transformation. We may even get a guy barging into our office at 10:00 p.m. demanding to be saved. Often, though, we never get to see the finished building. Still, we simply try to be faithful to what God is stirring in us and what the Spirit is doing through us at that particular time. We assume that God is "already in progress" in this person's life, and simply join Him there—listening, speaking, connecting, serving, and loving them toward Christ.

Jesus is up to something in the grey. May He give us eyes to see it and the power and presence of His Spirit to come alongside others with His truth and grace. May He stretch you, empower you, move you, and bless you along the way.

CONSIDER THIS
Already in Progress

1. "Jesus is up to something?" What do you sense He might be up to in you? Around you? Through you?

2. Do you truly believe that God has been at work in others, and will continue to be at work in them as you love on them and share your life with them? Why is that sometimes hard to believe?

3. Pick ten people that you most likely will come in contact with this week (neighbors, co-workers, class-mates, the lady who is always at the bus stop, home-less guy asking for a quarter, favorite barista, etc.).

4. Now what would it look like to come alongside each of them this week with the thought that Jesus is "up to something"?

5. What would it look like to plant or water, to listen to their story or frustrations, to serve in a specific way that meets a specific need, to speak in a way that is both encouraging and in alignment with truth and grace, to connect them with others, to apply Jesus' Story to their story?

6. What will a sense of urgency look like for you? A sense of freedom?

MAY HE STRETCH YOU,
EMPOWER YOU,
MOVE YOU,
AND BLESS YOU
ALONG THE WAY.

ACKNOWLEDGMENTS

For Campus House, this is our first venture into the book world, and it has been a collective effort from start to finish. Thanks to the GreyMob staff for putting the pieces together: Jason for the encouragement to write and helping frame the project, extraordinary designers Garrett and Emily for making it look amazing, and Amanda for fine tuning the details. I am very grateful for Beth, Olivia, and my wife, Lea, for doing the first read-throughs and our editor, Alice, for going the extra mile. Thanks to Jaclyn who contributed great ideas for discussion questions and to Abby, Richard, Doc, Diane, and others who helped refine some thoughts along the way. Many thanks to Dana, Ken, Shockey, Kevin, Ali, and our whole Campus House / Greyhouse / GreyMob staff team as well as the incredible Campus House students who encapsulate the art of "coming alongside" every day. Finally, I would like to express my appreciation to my family: my parents for their example, my sisters for their encouragement, my children for their inspiration, and my wife for her love and the way she stretches me to go deeper in faith, life, and ministry instead of just... further.

Thanks for reading. You can follow our collective, ongoing story at pcch.org, greyhousecoffee.com, and greymob.com.

CPSIA information can be obtained at www.ICGtesting.com
Printed in the USA
LVOW01s1822200314

378193LV00008B/23/P